STARBRITE TRAVELER

A TRAVEL RESOURCE FOR PARENTS OF CHILDREN WITH SPECIAL NEEDS

Written by Jesemine Jones and Ida Keiper
Consultant Emily A. Jones

DISCLAIMER

This book is not intended as a substitute for the medical advice of physicians. The reader should regularly consult a physician in matters relating to his/her health and the health of his/her child and more particularly alert the physician to any symptoms that may require diagnosis or medical attention.

Although the authors have made every effort to ensure that the information in this book is correct at press time, the authors and publisher do not assume and hereby disclaim any liability to any party for any loss, damage, or disruption caused by errors or omissions, whether such errors or omissions arise from negligence, accident, or any other cause. While every effort has been made to offer current and accurate information, this book may contain reference to certain policies, standards, and regulations that may change over time. Always confirm critical information prior to travel and seek professional advice when appropriate.

We do not endorse, represent or warrant the accuracy or reliability of any of the information, content, advertisements or other materials contained on, distributed through, or linked, downloaded or accessed from us. We do not endorse, represent or warrant the quality of any products, information or other materials displayed, purchased, or obtained as a result of or in connection with our service, and we do not endorse, represent or warrant the service, security or practices of any of the vendors whose products or services are included in our service. Any reliance upon any information, content, advertisements, materials, products, services or vendors included in or found through our service shall be at the user's sole risk.

DEDICATION

This book is dedicated to parents and caregivers of children with special needs.

Our vision is for children with disabilities to be treated with dignity and respect, afforded the same opportunities to live their lives to the fullest extent possible, and supported by society with sensitivity and compassion. We named our books *Starbrite Traveler* because we believe children are stars. We want children with special needs to explore new places giving them the confidence to embark on the journey of life. They are stars in our eyes. Our dream to help children and their families became a reality in 2011 when we created the Starbrite Kids Program.

Jesemine Jones and Ida Keiper, founders of Starry Night Travel, LLC created the Starbrite Kids Program specializing in arranging travel for children with special needs. Our staff is dedicated to providing families of children with special needs the help and support needed to make travel not only possible, but rewarding and enriching.

Starbrite Kids Travel, LLC donates a portion of the proceeds of this book to children's charities.

TABLE OF CONTENTS

Address travel concerns, change behavior and teach new skills by using evidenced based strategies for children with a variety of special needs: developmental disabilities, sensory processing disorder, and physical disabilities

*If I could reach up and hold a Star
for every time you made me smile,
the entire evening sky
would be in the palm of my hands.*
--Anonymous

PREFACE

The smile on Emma's face and the twinkle in her eyes conveyed what she was unable to say as she intently studied Cinderella's castle. For years, Emma's parents had wanted to fulfill their daughter's dream to visit the Magic Kingdom at Disney World. Due to her significant medical and ambulatory concerns, her parents thought that a trip requiring long-distance travel was not feasible. Emma has spastic quadriplegic CP, is nonverbal, and is fed through a gastrostomy tube. Emma's parents were overwhelmed by the supports that would be required prior to travel and while on vacation.

Emma's nurse provided Emma's mother, Natalie, with information about the Starbrite Kids Program, to help families of children with special needs plan vacations. In April 2012, Emma and her family traveled to Disney World.

Extensive planning by the Starbrite Kids staff and a little bit of fairy dust was necessary to make Emma's dream trip come true. On a mild day in April, Emma visited the Magical World of Disney. It was magical! Yes, all of Emma's disabilities were still there, but having everything so accommodating and seeing the smile on Emma's face made it all worthwhile. --Natalie

Starbrite Traveler: A Travel Resource for Parents of Children with Special Needs is written for all the Emma's in the world and their families. Our book was conceived and written, drawing from our fifty years of combined experience in the field of special education. Working with parents, we were repeatedly told how difficult it was for families with a child with special needs to travel. The greatest fear of many parents is that their child would not be able to handle the physical and/or emotional challenges of traveling. They feared the stress and transitions would be more than the child or parent could handle. Hearing these concerns combined with our belief that travel is a valuable experience for children, contributed to our desire to write this book.

We are dedicated to providing families of children with special needs the help and support needed to make travel not only possible, but a rewarding and enriching experience. Our Starbrite Kids Program advocates for children by fostering awareness within the travel industry so children and families are afforded the same opportunity to travel, see new places, and enjoy enriching experiences as other children.

Fortunately, over the past two decades, accessibility for individuals has improved with the passing of the Americans Disability Act of 1990, making travel more accessible for individuals with disabilities. Recently, numerous service providers (e.g., hotels, air carriers, attractions) have begun implementing sensitivity training for their staff to promote empathy and better support children with special needs. By providing appropriate services and special provisions, all children can successfully navigate the world just as their peers without disabilities.

Too often we underestimate the power of a touch, a smile, a kind word, a listening ear, an honest compliment, or the smallest act of caring, all of which have the potential to turn a life around.
– Leo Buscaglia

Although every child's disability is unique, social awareness and community connectedness are primary concerns that link parents. While traveling, there will be times when people around you do not understand your child's disability, especially if your child has an invisible disability. They may make unkind remarks or improper facial expressions. Instead of becoming upset, present them with this card, created for you by the Starbrite Kids Program:

★★
My child is a S.T.A.R.brite traveler

Please show
-*Sensitivity:* My child is the same as you but with a disability.
-*Tolerance:* Understand if my child does not act or look like you.
-*Awareness:* Ask questions if you want to know more about
 my child.
-*Respect:* My child is a human being with feelings.
★★

ACKNOWLEDGEMENTS

This book could not have been written without the support of the many wonderful parents, caregivers, and children we have had the privilege of knowing over the past thirty years; specifically, to Natalie, Amy, Amber, Cat, Kim, and Mary Pat for their insight and willingness to share their lives and personal experiences.

A special note of thanks goes to our consultant, Dr. Emily A. Jones, for her support, professional expertise, and unerring abilities. We thank Davy Rosenzweig for her zeal, and commitment to the subject of the book; Victor Calise, Matthew Puvogel, and the staff of Mayor Bloomberg's Office for their incredible knowledge, support, and commitment to children and families with disabilities; Carmen Berry for her enthusiasm, dedication, and focus throughout the process of putting our book together; Joseph Romano and Rich Loniewski of Monmouth County SCORE for their invaluable guidance and support for the past two years; Vito DeSantis, Director of the Commission of the Blind, for his candor, incredible wisdom, and kindness; Larry Wenig and Kim Goodwyn who was extremely helpful providing information regarding individuals who are deaf or hard of hearing; Chris Church for his talent in designing our cover; Our sisters for their deep commitment to children and their welfare; Jordan Breslauer for his marketing acumen; Enrique Cabrera for his Web expertise; Trish Drobish for her assistance; Sheldon and Janet Rock for their support and perception; Lori Gannon for her contribution; Colin Chapin for his keen editing eye, and Nicole Neil for her feedback and assistance with the final editing.

* * *

I would like to thank my mom, Lois, for her constant love and always believing in me. She is the best PR person a daughter can ask for. I also want to thank my husband, Doug, for his insight and continuous love and support; and my sons, Christopher and Kyle, for filling my life with love and laughter. Furthermore, I would like to thank my dad, Tony, for telling me since I was a little girl that I can do anything I put my mind to. I still feel his presence guiding me every day. —Ida

* * *

I wish to thank Roger, my husband, for his compassion, brilliance, commitment, and unwavering support of my passion. I also want to thank my daughter, Briana, for sharing her amazing creativity and wit as well as her encouragement every step of the way and my mother, Elizabeth, for her steadfast support, love, and belief in our dream. —Jesemine

Twenty years from now you will be more disappointed by the things you didn't do than by the ones you did do. So throw off the bowlines. Sail away from the safe harbor. Catch the trade winds in your sails. Explore. Dream. Discover.
—Mark Twain

INTRODUCTION

Our book, *Starbrite Traveler: A Travel Resource for Parents of Children with Special Needs* was written for parents, caregivers, relatives, and friends of children with special needs to help them plan an enjoyable vacation. Whether your child has had limited travel experience, has traveled extensively or has experience somewhere in between, our book has something for everyone.

Starbrite Traveler is divided into five chapters to reflect the 5 D's of planning for successful travel: Dream, Determine, Dry Run, Departure, and Destination. We recommend that you read each chapter in order, as they build upon each other. Throughout the book, we include vignettes from parents sharing their concerns and their successful travel experiences. We also include shared insight and wisdom from adults with special needs and the importance of travel for children.

Our book is unique in that we welcome you to contact us at starbritetraveler@gmail.com to share and gain valuable information from other parents and our staff.

Chapter 1

First you ***Imagine your Dream Vacation.*** We discuss dreaming about the type of trip you want to take. Think about where you and your family have always wanted to go and DREAM. To help you with this process, we include a "Family Interest Planner." The advantages and disadvantages of vacation options including cruises, lodging at all-inclusive resorts, large hotels, small venues, vacation rentals, camping, and ski resorts are discussed. We provide an overview of the many activities and attractions your entire family can enjoy on vacation, including theme/amusement parks, zoos, aquariums, museums, beaches, and events.

Chapter 2

In ***Determine Special Provisions Required Prior to Travel*** we include information about special provisions and accessibility for a child with ambulatory or medical needs, visual impairments, is deaf or hard of hearing, and/or has special dietary needs. For each area of need, we discuss special provisions, accessibility, and tips for cruising, accommodations, attractions, and modes of transportation. To help identify special provisions for transportation, accommodations, and attractions use our "Special Needs Pre-Trip Questionnaire." At the end of this chapter you will have considered your dreams, your child's needs, and the advantages and disadvantages of various types of travel and attractions to determine the best trip for your family.

Chapter 3

In ***Dry Run: Pre-Travel Rehearsal*** we discuss common travel concerns for children with special needs. Concerns may center on getting ready for vacation, different modes of transportation, interacting with others, and staying safe. The Starbrite Kids Three Step method will help you identify potential travel concerns before you go on vacation. For each area of concern, suggested strategies help prepare you and your child for vacation. The strategies have an evidence-base to change behavior and/or teach new skills to children with a variety of disabilities. We walk you through the steps to apply the strategy and provide activities to practice with your child before and during your vacation. To address safety, we include interactive illustrated scenarios and activities to teach and reinforce safety with your child.

Chapter 4

In ***Travel Essentials for Departure*** we provide you with a timeline to guide you in planning for your vacation, as well as a packing checklist to ensure you are prepared for your trip.

Chapter 5

The final step is ***Destination: Arrival*** where we focus on making sure all last minute details are in place. We offer tips and reminders before going to attractions. Remember to have fun and create lasting memories!

Note
In an effort to make our book more reader friendly we are using the pronoun he to refer to both he and she. In some of our drawings we refer to Jamie as being male to keep continuity throughout the book, however you are welcome to consider Jamie female. We are careful to avoid gender bias in our drawings. Adapt them to your family's composition. We want all of our readers to identify with the information in our book.

MY FAMILY

REALITY – ALL FAMILIES

Benefits of Travel

All children benefit from travel. Vito DeSantis, Director of the New Jersey Commission for the Blind and Visually Impaired, is an avid traveler who does not let his visual impairment hold him back. He and his wife have traveled to Utah, Montana, Wyoming, and Alaska where they have enjoyed kayaking, skiing, hiking, and mountain climbing.

> Vito believes, *"Parents should allow their children to experience what other children experience to help them feel more confident. The opportunity to travel is important to help prepare children to become independent adults."*

Travel provides family time together while creating lasting memories
Vacationing as a family helps families reconnect without the pressure of daily stressors such as school, work, and the responsibilities of running a household. Your child may not remember if you stayed at a five-star hotel or dined in a world-renowned restaurant, but he will remember the time you spent together.

Travel exposes your child to the world
Traveling to new places gives your child the chance to experience different cultures, foods, geography, and climates. Even small trips to nearby cities and attractions can provide your child with new opportunities.

Travel provides opportunities to practice and improve social and communication skills
Travel provides opportunities to interact and communicate with new people. Your child will meet people from various professions such as flight attendants, taxi drivers, and hotel staff. He may also meet people from other regions and countries, gaining experience with language and cultural differences.

Ida recalls a trip she took with her son: *"I still remember when my son was playing with a child from France in a pool in Mexico. They could not understand each other's language, but they created a game so they taught each other how to count in their native language. As they counted and arrived at a certain number they would jump in the pool."*

Travel provides opportunities to be outdoors and increase physical activity level

Traveling often involves time spent outside, enjoying the fresh air, and reaping the benefits of nature. A growing body of research supports the benefits of connecting with nature. Experiencing nature may help self-confidence, increase curiosity, enhance learning, improve cognitive functioning and creativity, promote good health, reduce aggression, and lower stress levels (White, 2012).

Travel stimulates a child's senses and contributes to cognitive growth

Traveling is full of teachable moments. We are firm believers that "experience is the best teacher." Children learn from hands-on experiences at children's museums, aquariums, and science centers. There is something special about going to a historic site and walking where others have walked in past eras. By exploring nature at state and national parks, your child will learn about geography and different cultures. Aquariums and caves are a great way for children to learn about what is in the sea and underground. Your child may not realize he is learning because the experience is so much fun!

DREAM
IMAGINE YOUR VACATION

What is your dream vacation?

Relax on a white-sandy beach
Hike off the beaten track
Visit an amusement park, zoo, or aquarium
Investigate a science or discovery museum
Appreciate the beauty of art, taste the cuisine of a foreign region
Tour an ancient ruin, visit an exciting city
Cruise, swim with the dolphins
Ski, camp, fish, explore state and national parks,
Dream

Planning a vacation begins with dreaming about where to go and what to do. Involve your entire family in dreaming about your vacation. This is a time for brainstorming vacation ideas, where everyone has the opportunity to express where they would like to go and what they would like to do on vacation.

Vacation options are numerous. We suggest narrowing the choices before having a conversation with your family about their dream vacation. First, decide on the location you would like to visit. Do you want to visit a tropical island, a foreign country, a small town in the country, a major city, or take a cruise? The options are endless! Certain factors will determine your destination. What is your allotted time frame and budget? Will you fly, drive, or take a train? What is the climate like? Are there attractions in the area that your children will enjoy? Do you need passports?

Once you have decided on a location for your vacation, you will still need to decide on your *accommodations* and attractions

> **Accommodations**
> - lodging

to visit. To help you with this process, our Family Interest Planner will give you an overview of what types of vacations are available. Fill in each family member's name at the top of the planner and put it aside for now.

Read about the advantages and disadvantages of different types of accommodations as well as an overview of various attractions in this chapter. Use this information to help you narrow down the type of vacation that will best meet the needs of your family. You may either highlight the vacation options on the planner or customize your own.

For example, Kim and John read the information in this chapter and reviewed the Family Interest Planner. They decided a trip to Chicago would be a great choice as they could visit family living in Chicago and take advantage of the attractions a big city has to offer. They plan on staying at a large hotel to enjoy the amenities and the convenient location. Kim and John created a Family Interest Planner with a list of attractions available in Chicago that they thought would be appropriate for their family. They chose a museum, zoo, aquarium, and science center. Under museums they listed the Chicago Children's Museum and the Museum of Science and Industry as options. Then they involved their children in the planning process by discussing available attraction options. Kim and John helped each of their children research the attractions. Each child then indicated his choices on the Family Interest Planner.

After everyone completes the planner, discuss the trip as a family and plan your vacation. At the end of this chapter you will have a tentative plan for your vacation that you will use in Chapter 2 to identify *special provisions,* and make final decisions about your vacation.

> *Special provisions* – appropriate supplies and devices for individuals with special needs, i.e. wheelchair accessibility, adaptive equipment, dietary needs, transportation, medical supplies, and oxygen

Family Interest Planner

	Parent	Parent	Child	Child	Other
USA Destinations					
City					
Small town					
Mountains					
Beachfront					
Foreign Destinations					
Country					
Island					

	Parent	Parent	Child	Child	Other
Accommoda-tions					
Cruise ship					
All inclusive resort					
Large hotel					
Small hotel					
Motel					
B&B					
Vacation rental - home/condo/villa					

	Parent	Parent	Child	Child	Other
Campsite					
Ski resort					
Attractions					
Aquariums					
Beaches					
Boundless Playgrounds					
Museums					
Theme/ amusement parks					

	Parent	Parent	Child	Child	Other
Zoos					
Events - sports/ concerts/ shows					
Other					

Go to starbritetravel.com to download this form.

Travel Accommodations

When choosing accommodations for your vacation you have several options: cruises, all-inclusive resorts, large hotels, small venues, vacation rentals, campsites, and ski resorts. Deciding on the right accommodation for your family depends on the type of vacation and the location you choose. For example, if you are visiting a beach location, an all-inclusive resort or large hotel may be the best choice for your family as they offer a wide array of activities for children. If you choose a city destination you may want to choose a smaller, less expensive hotel in the area, since you will be spending most time sightseeing. If you want to sail the seven seas, choose a cruise, an all-inclusive floating resort that leaves from and visits ports all over the world. The cruise ship becomes your transportation, lodging, and entertainment. In this section we provide you with a description of each type of accommodation, including their advantages and disadvantages. Choose the accommodations based on your family's interests and needs.

Cruises

Cruises can last from three nights to an entire year and stop in multiple ports; giving passengers a taste of different locations. If this is you or your child's first cruise, choose a shorter one such as "a cruise to nowhere," that goes out to sea for a day. Another option is a day excursion that will take you and your family on a small boat lasting a few hours. Day cruises include whale watching, sightseeing around cities and lakes, fishing tours, snorkeling expeditions, and duck tours (land and water). Day cruises tend to be economical and accessible. They offer an excellent option to prepare your child for a longer cruise. You will gain insight into how your child adjusts to this new environment before committing to a longer trip.

At *ports of call,* cruise lines offer a variety of shore excursions for different ability levels and interests. Snorkel through

Ports of call – any of the ports at which a ship will be stopping on a cruise

coral reefs, explore ancient ruins, shop local markets, or explore tropical islands and exotic countries. You have these options along with the convenience of returning to the cruise ship to dine and sleep. Passengers may purchase excursions through their cruise line, travel consultant, or book on their own. It is recommended to book prior to sailing, as some excursions sell out quickly.

The price of the cruise includes transportation from port to port, lodging, meals, and entertainment. Many *amenities* are *standard* on cruises, such as children's programs, kids pools, water slides, sports courts, arcades, crafts, games, and shows. Other services and activities may involve an additional expense. Expenses you need to consider are tipping, personal expenditures, baby-sitting, medical fees, beauty shop, laundry, and dry cleaning. Liquor and soft drinks are also extra on most cruises. Port charges, transportation to and from the *embarkation point,* and *shore excursions* are also extra costs.

> *Amenities* – comforts and conveniences
> *Standard* – services usually found on most cruise ships and hotels
> *Embarkation point* – where you board the ship
> *Shore excursions* – organized land based trips on a cruise

Cruises range dramatically in price depending on the cruise line, length of trip, and time of year. Peak season for Caribbean cruising is from mid-December to mid-April. Storms and hurricanes are more prevalent in the Caribbean in the summer and fall. Plan accordingly if you travel off-season. In contrast, cruises up the Alaskan coast are most popular during summer months.

Some cruise lines have special programs for children. These programs provide entertainment and social activities for your child. Before deciding on a cruise and cruise line, check out the children's programs to find out which cruises will offer your child the best experience.

Advantages of cruises

- Pack and unpack only once
- Entertainment and activities
- Mealtime seating is prearranged
- Laundry and dry cleaning services
- Library and cinema
- Infirmary with medical personnel
- Opportunities to visit many sites of interest, such as islands, attractions, and historical locations
- Duty free shops on the ship and often at ports of call
- Pre-payment of trip
- *Priority boarding* and *disembarking*
- *Private muster drills*
- *Special equipment* can be delivered directly to the ship
- Wheelchair accessible cabins and decks
- Special dietary meals
- *Orientation tours* for those who are visually impaired or deaf or hard of hearing

---

Priority boarding – first group of people to board a ship or airplane

Disembarking – getting off the ship

Private muster drills – a safety demonstration conducted by members of the ship's staff that instructs passengers on the use of a life preserver and other important safety information – individuals who have difficulty with loud noises or crowds will be taken to an alternate quiet location on the ship

Special equipment –wheelchair, walker, TTY device

Orientation tours – a tour of the public spaces

Visual/tactile alert kits – kits that include special equipment that can be installed in your hotel room or cabin to ensure that individuals who are deaf or hard of hearing will be alerted if someone knocks on the door, the telephone rings, or a smoke detector goes off

---

- *Visual/tactile alert kits*, closed caption television, and sign language interpreters are available
- Special needs access desk on-board the ship
- Special needs brochures detailing amenities and programs offered
- Children's programs may accommodate special needs

Mara and her mother, Susan, take a cruise every year. Susan reports every cruise line is different and that each cruise has its own advantages and disadvantages for those who use wheelchairs. Susan recommends booking newer ships that have wheelchair-accessible staterooms with wider doorframes, handrails, accessible furniture and closets, low sinks, and wheel-in showers. Susan says, "Every cruise we have taken has been wonderful. The staff has always been very accommodating and helpful towards ... passengers [with disabilities]."
--S.W., New York

Disadvantages of cruises
- Seasickness
- Small cabins can limit mobility
- Narrow hallways for wheelchair users
- Lines to wait for meals and excursions
- Limited time at each port (6-8 hours)
- Noise and crowds
- Expense of excursions and other extras
- Children's activities vary from cruise-to-cruise for children with special needs
- Limited numbers of cabins for wheelchair accessibility

★ **Tips**

If none of the excursions appeal to you, stay on the ship and enjoy a day of fun and relaxation.

Many ships offer spa discounts on days when the ship is docked!

Crewmembers suggest eating a green apple with salt to alleviate nausea.

Cruise ships have stabilizers that extend from both sides of the ship to minimize roll and seasickness. If you have never cruised and are prone to motion sickness, you may want to take precautions. Speak to your physician prior to your trip to discuss options.

All-Inclusive Resorts

Most all-inclusive resorts are designed specifically for families. They tend to have multiple amenities and activities, including pools, water parks, *motorized* and *non-motorized* water equipment, arcades, and children's programs. Resorts are usually in locations with breathtaking views of the ocean or mountains. Planning your vacation may be less stressful since all-inclusive resorts charge one price that covers meals,

> *Motorized* – equipment with a motor (e.g., jet ski)
> *Non-motorized* – equipment without a motor (e.g., snorkel, boogie board)

entertainment, sports, lodging, tips, and most activities. In addition, shuttle transfers to and from the airport are usually included. For the few times you may want to leave the complex, use a resort shuttle or taxi.

At large all-inclusive chain resorts you can often take advantage of exchange privileges. This means you can use the amenities and restaurants available at resorts affiliated with the one at which you are staying.

Larger resorts may be overwhelming with many activities and lots of people. Staying at a small all-inclusive resort may be less crowded, however, amenities and restaurant choices may be limited. The decision between a large or small resort may depend on how well your child deals with stimulation and choices. Your child may enjoy a smaller, less action-packed atmosphere, a larger and exciting experience, or somewhere in between.

Recently, we helped Jennifer take her children, one of whom has special needs, on vacation to an island resort. Considering her family's needs and vacation dreams, her family traveled to Punta Cana in the Dominican Republic. She described her experience:

"I have three children ranging from three to nine years old. My six-year old son ... [has autism]. With the help of the staff at Starbrite, I decided to stay at a small all-inclusive resort. I wanted the benefits of an all-inclusive, but needed a resort that was quiet, hoping to have a calming effect on my son. Staying at the resort was perfect. The day-to-day transitions were minimal, since we usually had the same servers in the restaurant and staff in the children's program. My son participated in the arts and craft projects and activities in the children's program."

"The restaurants were accommodating to my son's gluten intolerance and milk allergy. The best part of staying at an all-inclusive resort is that there is something to do for everyone in the family. My husband and I were able to have a little down time in addition to time with each of our children while the others were involved in activities. It is important to note the success of this trip was due to pre-planning by the Starbrite staff, i.e. conversations with hotel management and restaurant staff prior to departure." --J.S., Florida

Advantages of all-inclusive resorts
- Convenience and safety since you do not have to leave the grounds
- Pack and unpack once
- *First class* or *deluxe accommodations*

- *Concierge* to assist with off-site excursions
- Scenic locales
- Multiple dining options
- Entertainment
- Pools and water parks
- Spas
- Beauty services
- Gift shops
- Wide range of activities for all ages (e.g., tennis, golf, skiing, water sports)
- Gives older children more freedom
- Kid's program and arcades
- Babysitting
- Laundry
- Housekeeping service
- Internet access
- Coffee maker, cable television in room
- Pay one rate for lodging, meals, and many activities (makes budgeting easy)
- Package deals can include airfare and round trip transfers from the airport to the resort
- Wheelchair accessible rooms
- Visual and tactile kits are available for children that are deaf and hard of hearing (Information found in Chapter 2)
- *Closed caption television*

> *First class* – a very good to excellent hotel
> *Deluxe accommodations* – luxurious hotel
> *Concierge* – staff member of a hotel or cruise ship whose function is to provide information and services to guests

> *Closed caption television* – dialogue from a television show appears in a black box at the bottom of the screen

Disadvantages of all-inclusive resorts
- Availability of special dietary meals varies (check resort)
- Boredom due to dining at the same place for all meals
- Reluctance to dine elsewhere because meals are pre-paid

- Alcohol, spa treatments, and some activities usually have an additional cost
- May be too expensive for large families
- Many are located in isolated spots away from major cities and hospitals
- Wheelchair accessibility, visual tactile kits, and closed caption television may be limited in smaller resorts

---

★ **Tips**

Before booking, be sure to ask:

What exactly is included in the quoted price?

Are there any special events?

Are drinks included in the price?

Is there a fitness room on the premises?

If so, is there an extra charge to use the facility?

Are there any discounts for travelers with disabilities?

Large Hotels

Large hotels consist of 200 to 300 or more rooms and usually offer a range of rooms including one and two bedroom suites for families. Suites are a convenient option for families since they provide more living space and amenities than standard hotel rooms. Living and bedroom areas are separate, providing privacy.

There is typically a common lobby area and rooms generally open directly into the hallway. Large hotels offer many amenities such as pools, game rooms, spas, fitness centers, and restaurants. You may have access to multiple restaurants as well as a cocktail lounge with entertainment.

Extended stay hotels – hotel with option to stay for weeks/months; amenities such as housekeeping service, laundry services are available

All suite – rooms with a separate sleeping and living area

Lodging can range from superior deluxe to moderate tourist class. Superior deluxe hotels may have high-quality linens, Jacuzzis, and upscale bath products. *Extended stay hotels* may offer an *all-suite* option, which includes a living room, sleeping, and kitchenette area. The hotel's location, room size, furnishings, occupancy, availability, and the time of the year determine the cost of the room. Business travelers often use large hotels during the week. As a result, bargain packages are offered to leisure travelers on the weekends and holidays.

Advantages of large hotels

- Multiple dining options/restaurants
- Pools
- Swim up bars
- Water parks
- Motorized and non-motorized water equipment
- Spas
- Beauty services
- Kid's spas
- Arcades
- Children's programs
- Tennis and basketball courts
- Golf
- Gift shops
- Nighttime entertainment
- Concierge service to assist with tours
- Internet access
- Coffee maker, refrigerator, cable television in room
- Housekeeping service
- Room service
- Babysitting
- Wheelchair accessible rooms
- Visual and tactile kits are available
- Closed caption television is available

Disadvantages of large hotels

- May or may not provide complimentary breakfast
- Usually more expensive than other lodging
- Room service is pricey

★ **Tips**

Before booking, ask:

    Is there parking at or near the hotel?
    Are parking fees included or extra?
    Are there dining facilities at the hotel?
    Is breakfast included in the room price?
    What is the early check-in and late checkout policy?
    What amenities are included in the room price?
    Is Internet access free at the hotel and in the room?
    Are there childcare services? If so, what is the minimum age requirement, staff experience with children with special needs, qualifications of provider, and cost?

Small Venues

If you are looking for a comfortable and clean environment with no frills, staying at a small venue may be the right choice for your family. There are many different types of small venues, most ranging from 25 to 100 rooms. This option is best for families who will be spending most of their vacation visiting attractions and less time in the room.

Small hotels tend to be quaint and charming and may be found in many towns and even in large cities. They offer fewer amenities than a large hotel. When traveling out of the country, accessibility varies and must be checked prior to travel. Some small European hotels may have only very small elevators with narrow entrances making it difficult for wheelchair users.

Motels are economical and suitable for short stays. Motels are usually two stories high with ample guest parking at the door. Motels are usually alongside the highway and therefore easily accessible. Motels offer limited dining options. Many have pools.

Bed and Breakfasts (B&Bs) are often the best choice for travelers looking for unique character and a taste of the local area. B&Bs tend to be homey and friendly, providing a family-type feel to your visit. However, privacy is sometimes sacrificed, as guests may have to share bathroom facilities. A second downside is that some do not allow children and have limited amenities. B&Bs are usually individually owned and operated. Check for wheelchair accessibility and other special provisions. Lodging abroad can go by different names; for example, in Europe, pensions are small family run lodges similar to B&Bs; upscale inns are called Chateaux, castles, or villas.

Advantages of small venues
- Less crowded
- Less overwhelming
- Offer more personal attention from staff
- Opportunity to sample local cuisine and culture
- Water equipment such as boogie boards, surfboards, paddle boats may be available
- Coffee maker, refrigerator, cable television and Internet service may be available
- Motels can be 1 or 2 stories with outside access to rooms
- Reasonable cancellation policy (24-48 hours prior to stay)
- Many have closed caption television and visual/hearing alerts

Disadvantages of small venues
- Limited amenities
- Rooms may be small
- May be costly for larger families - required to book more than one room i.e. many B&Bs only permit 2 people in a room and most small hotels only permit 4 people in a room
- May have shared bathrooms (B&Bs)

- No children's program
- Often no dining, other than breakfast
- No nightly entertainment
- Limited housekeeping service
- No room service
- No transfers to/from the airport/hotel
- Wheelchair accessible rooms are not always available

★ Tips

If your budget permits, book a larger room or suite, preferably with a kitchenette or at minimum, a microwave and mini refrigerator. The extra space will make it easier to navigate suitcases and special equipment such as a wheelchair. A larger room also allows for a play area and/or private space for your child.

Choose the location of your hotel or resort in relation to the activities you will be enjoying. For a beach vacation, try to stay close to the beach so walking is possible. This avoids driving, traffic, parking, packing, and unpacking. Try to make it easier for yourself whenever possible.

To minimize noise, ask for a room away from elevators or noisy street side of the hotel.

For a larger family, booking two connecting hotel rooms is usually less expensive than booking a 2-bedroom suite. When booking, ask the resort or hotel to send you a written confirmation that the rooms are guaranteed to be connecting to avoid any unwanted surprises when you arrive at the hotel.

Vacation Rentals

Vacation rentals include private homes, villas, and condominiums (condos). Rentals are perfect for a family vacation when privacy and flexibility are important. Locations include beachfront homes/condos, country homes, and cabins in the woods. Vacation rentals are available for all budgets. Rentals offer the option to prepare your own snacks and meals and provide more space than hotels. Private homes, villas, and condos are individually owned and usually rented out certain times of the year. If there are multiple units in a rental, check on the condition of the unit by asking if it has been recently renovated. A real estate agent can help you find the best option for your family, or you can search online.

Another option is a vacation home exchange. Swapping homes with other families with similar special needs is a low-cost and practical alternative. You can verify in advance how accessible the vacation home is by speaking with the owner.

Advantages of rentals

- Multiple bedrooms and bathrooms
- Ample room to accommodate a family with special equipment
- Ability to prepare your own meals
- Quiet surroundings and privacy
- Ability to choose amenities (e.g., fireplace, Jacuzzi, hot tub, swimming pool)
- Pets may be permitted
- Electronic equipment such as stereos, game systems, and computers may be available
- Cost may be less than booking two or more hotel rooms for a large family

Disadvantages of rentals

- Most do not offer daily housekeeping service (there may be an additional charge for cleaning when you leave)
- Stringent cancellation policy (maybe 30 days)
- May need to bring bed linens, towels, and other household items
- May be disappointed by the condition of the property
- No *support staff* on site if problems arise

> ***Support staff*** – reservation desk, concierge, valet, and housekeeping

- Limited wheelchair accessible rooms and hallways may be narrow

Camping and Campsites

Camping is an outdoor recreational activity that is enjoyed by many families. Camping gives children the opportunity to discover their environment and learn new

> **Campground** – an outdoor area for setting up camp
> **Recreational vehicle (RV)** - a large vehicle used for camping

skills. There is something special about being surrounded by the natural beauty of our country, whether going for a day trip to a national park or sleeping under the stars at a *campground.*

A variety of campsites are available throughout the country, ranging from basic tent sites with minimal amenities, to *recreational vehicle (RV)* sites that have many amenities. Cabins, cottages, and luxury lodging are available for an upscale camping experience.

Camping in national parks is one way to enjoy the waterfalls, glaciers, wildlife, and mountains. The National Park Service, U.S. Department of the Interior, provides a variety of programs and information for visitors. Campers enjoy activities such as fishing, swimming, biking, canoeing, and hiking. Whenever possible, the same opportunities are provided for visitors with disabilities. For more information about national parks visit www.nps.gov.

Advantages of camping
- Activities such as fishing, hiking, swimming are on site
- Usually near woods, mountains, or lakes
- Affordable
- Some sites are free
- Provides numerous benefits of being exposed to nature

Disadvantages of camping

- Facilities and amenities are limited
- Limited cell phone signal
- Limited electricity
- Insects
- Poison ivy
- Quality of accommodations varies from facility to facility

★ Tips

If you are tent camping, practice putting up your tent in your backyard before leaving home to ensure all pieces are intact and in good condition.

Bring your own first aid kit and bug spray.

For an extensive list of camping health and safety tips visit the Department of Health and Human Resources – Center for Disease Control and Prevention at www.cdc.gov/family/camping/

Skiing and Ski Resorts

"Skiing has always been a big part of our lives. Our family spends every weekend on the slopes in New Hampshire. Our dream was to include my daughter, Margot, who has physical and motor delays with muscle weakness and poor balance. We were thrilled to find an adaptive ski program at Loon Mountain. The staff at New England Disabled Sports has been fabulous motivators for Margot and our entire family. It was a thrill to see Margot up on skis during her first lesson. She is so excited that she can now ski with her brother and sisters. In fact, she is usually the first one dressed and ready to go hit the slopes in the early morning. I feel that learning how to ski not only increased Margot's balance and agility, but has greatly improved her self-confidence."
– A.U., Massachusetts

All family members can enjoy winter sports. Activities at ski resorts include *alpine skiing, cross-country skiing*, snowboarding, tubing, and snowshoeing. You can spend the day at a ski resort enjoying the activities they have to offer for the day or stay overnight at the resort or a hotel nearby. Lodging at the resort tends to be expensive, however the convenience may be worth the extra cost. Meals and snacks are available including a variety of food service options ranging from cafeteria style to sit down dining.

> *Alpine skiing* – downhill skiing
> *Cross-country skiing* – skiing across the countryside

> *Adaptive skiing* – skiing using special equipment
> *Mono-skis* – a bucket style seat with a single ski underneath it
> *Bi-skis* – a bucket style seat with two skis underneath it
> *Sliders* – a type of ski mounted to a walker

Many ski resorts also offer *adaptive skiing* and snowboarding programs for children and adults with special needs. Adaptive equipment including *mono-skis, bi-skis,* and *sliders* are available. Call the ski resort in advance and speak with an adaptive ski instructor to arrange lessons and special equipment rentals. Additionally, many ski resorts offer camps and other programs for children with special needs. Activities include sleigh riding, dog sledding, alpine and cross-country skiing, horseback riding, and ice-skating. Since enrollment may be limited, call the ski resort in advance to reserve a spot for your child.

Skiing offers many benefits. It improves motor skills including balance and coordination, increases strength, and builds confidence and self-esteem.

Advantages of ski resorts
- Ski school for all ages
- Many offer adaptive ski programs
- Child care facilities

- Game rooms
- Option to rest when needed
- Ability to prepare snack/meals in room
- Rental equipment is available
- Ski-shops to purchase apparel
- Restaurants on premises
- Excellent hot chocolate!

Disadvantages of ski resorts
- Poor weather conditions may limit time on the slopes
- High altitude sickness
- Expensive (equipment rental fees, lift tickets, and lodging)
- Noisy and overcrowded during holiday season

★ Tips

Rent ski equipment at home before heading to the slopes to avoid long lines.

Make sure ski boots fit properly.

Enroll your child in lessons (skiing, snowboarding) at the resort. Arrive early to complete required paperwork.

We live in a wonderful world that is full of beauty, charm and adventure. There is no end to the adventures we can have if only we seek them with our eyes open.
– Jawaharal Nehru

Adventure Vacations

Adventure vacations focus on outdoor activities such as horseback riding, camel riding, biking, canoeing, sailing, rafting, skiing, tennis, scuba diving, and snorkeling. Depending on the activity, adventure vacations are classified as hard or soft. Hard adventures feature strenuous activities such as kayaking or mountain climbing. These often take place in remote locations and may be risky. We advise against these for anyone but the most experienced adventurers. In contrast, soft adventures involve activities that offer less challenge or danger such as walking, hiking, fishing, and boating. Visiting natural water slides and panning for gems, crystals, and fossils can also be great fun. Some activities may require adaptive equipment to ensure your child's safety.

There are many benefits of outdoor activity and connecting with nature. In addition to the obvious health benefits, time spent in nature offer more subtle benefits.

- It does not take much time in nature to enjoy the benefits--30 minutes can have a positive psychological impact (Kaplan & Kaplan, 1989).
- Outdoor activities such as hiking may enhance creativity and improve problem solving (Strayer, Atchley, & Atchley, 2012).
- Motor fitness, especially balance and coordination, is strengthened through outdoor activities. Playgrounds are a natural setting for your child to increase motor skills (Fjortoft, 2001).
- According to one study (Wells & Evan, 2003) exposure to nature helps alleviate and buffer stress for children. In fact, the more time spent outdoors; the better children were able to manage stress and challenges.

When children get a little older, they need to be exposed to many different things to stimulate their continued learning in different areas of life.
--Temple Grandin

Attractions

In addition to dreaming about where you will be going and where you will be staying, think about the activities your family would enjoy. The choice of activities will depend on your destination. For example, if you decide to go to a ski resort, you will likely be skiing, and snowboarding.

Important Information
For destinations and attractions that are special needs friendly, check out, *Starbrite Traveler: Destinations for Kids with Special Needs - East Coast Edition* (See summary in back of book).

Aquariums

Experience a delightful place where you can see colorful sea creatures swimming almost close enough to touch. Aquariums are a great place to take your entire family on a day trip. Parents, grandparents, and children will find aquariums educational and relaxing.

Most aquariums have touch tanks where children are provided a hands-on experience. For added fun, many aquariums offer behind the scenes aquarium tours to learn about how the aquarium staff cares for and feeds the animals. At some aquariums there are opportunities to swim with dolphins. Download a list of events and map of the aquarium prior to leaving home.

As with many attractions, purchasing tickets ahead of time by phone or through the aquarium Web site can help avoid waiting in long lines.

Beaches

Visiting the beach can be part of a great vacation. Spend time playing in the sand and swimming in the ocean. Try boogie boarding or surfing. For people with mobility issues, the sand can be tricky to navigate, however many beaches throughout the United States provide accessibility.

To make going to the beach accessible for those who use a cane or wheelchair, some beaches are equipped with wooden pathways and beach mats. These paths are laid on the sand and extend to the high tide water line permitting the safe use of a wheelchair or cane to navigate the sand. Additionally, manual and power beach wheelchairs are available upon request at many beach hotels, beach shops, or specialty surf shops. For more information on beach wheelchairs, see Chapter 2. For water safety activities, see Chapter 3.

★ **Tip**

Sun and heat exposure are potential issues when outdoors. Drink plenty of water to avoid heat exhaustion and sunstroke. Use sunscreen to prevent sunburn and a hat and sun-visor to protect your head and eyes from the sun. Closed shoes can prevent sunburn on your feet and protect your feet from injuries. Wearing a wet suit can provide insulation, extra cushioning, and protection from sun exposure. For dehydration and heat exhaustion prevention see Appendix 2 Heat Safety.

★ **Tip**

When boating and participating in water sports, children should wear U.S. Coast Guard approved life jackets. Visit www.safekids. org for information on how to choose the right life jacket for your child.

Boundless Playgrounds™

Play is essential for a child's social, emotional, and cognitive development. Play promotes creativity and imagination along with gross motor skills.

Boundless Playgrounds™, Inc. is the nation's leading nonprofit developer of truly inclusive playgrounds where children – and adults – of all abilities can play and learn together in a fun and welcoming environment. There are nearly 200 Boundless playgrounds in over 30 states and Canada with 100 more currently under development.

Boundless Playgrounds™ go beyond the requirements of the American Disability Act. The playgrounds address the needs of children with different physical, developmental, cognitive, and sensory abilities.

Interesting Fact
Play is so important to optimal child development that it has been recognized as a right of every child by the United Nations High Commission for Human Rights (General Assembly Resolution, 1989).

Boundless Playgrounds ™ include
- Ramped wheelchair access to the highest platform center
- Universally accessible pathways and surfacing
- Activity transfers that maximize accessibility
- Play structures that support child development
- Swings and equipment with back support
- Elevated sand tables and activity panels
- Activities for the hearing and visually impaired

For more information, visit www.boundlessplaygrounds.org

Museums

Museums are a great place to take children of all ages. Children can explore physical and natural sciences, history, world culture, and the arts. The interests and abilities of your child will determine what type of museum you choose. There are many different museums:

- Spy museums can be the perfect place to visit if your child is intrigued with spy games. Your child will become involved in top-secret activities, including how to break a code and use high tech gadgets.
- Space museums are a treat for the science buff.
- Transportation museums specialize in cars, trains, boats, space ships, planes, and skateboards.
- Art museums offer galleries filled with historical art from the ancient past to current modern art. Since exhibits change throughout the year, a repeat visit can be scheduled.
- History museums tell the stories of the past. There are large museums devoted to historical displays around the world spanning hundreds of years. Often small towns have museums focused on the birthplace of a famous person, a ghost town, or the location of a Civil War battle.
- Botanical gardens and arboretums offer a unique collection of trees, plants, and flowers from all over the world to amaze and awe.
- Specialty museums are available around the country. Visit wax museums, stuffed animal and doll museums, musical instrument museums, radio museums, and even museums about cartoon characters. Whatever your child's interests may be, there is one out there!
- Children's museums cater to children with shows, interactive hands-on exhibits, and rest areas with toys and games.

Theme/Amusement Parks

Theme or amusement parks bring out the child in all of us. They offer an abundance of activities that appeal to the entire family and children of all ages. There are hundreds of parks around the country. Experience huge ground shaking rides or for the less adventurous, enjoy the Ferris wheel, merry–go–round, arcade games, and entertainment.

Many parks offer accessibility guides on their Web site outlining the special provisions provided for rides and shows. For children with a physical disability, some rides are wheelchair accessible. In the event they are not, you can transfer your child onto the ride using a sliding bench if one is available at the park. For an ultra wheelchair accessible park, Morgan's Wonderland in San Antonio, Texas is the place to visit.

Theme/amusement parks often provide:
- Plenty of places to eat and rest
- Activities for the entire family
- Special dietary meals or the option to bring your own food
- Discounts for individuals with special needs – you will need a physician's note outlining disability
- Lodging at the facility or nearby
- *Guest assistance pass* for individuals with disabilities

> *Guest assistance pass* – a pass that provides assistance or special provisions for individuals with disabilities. The pass may provide:
> - A different entrance to access rides with possibly a shorter line and a shaded spot
> - A seat up front at shows

Zoos

Chicago, New York, and Philadelphia are home to the first zoos in the United States. Today, there are hundreds of zoos in the United States, giving families from all over the nation access to this attraction. Zoos give children the opportunity to see wildlife from all over the world. Zoos create a wonderful educational and fun environment for children of all ages; teaching them about nature, animals, the environment, endangered species, and conservation.

Many zoos throughout the country have programs for children with special needs. These may include live animal presentations and multi-sensory hands-on activities. Feeding times, a list of animals housed at the facility, and special programs can be found on most Web sites.

Zoos can be extremely large. Download a map of the zoo and review with your child his "must see" animals so you can prioritize your visit. Trying to see everything can be exhausting for you and your child. If possible, visiting a large zoo on two days may be easier.

Tigers and lions tend to sleep a lot, so the best time to see them is in the morning when they are most active. Semi-aquatic animals, including polar bears and hippos will often begin their morning with a swim. If the zoo has an underwater viewing center, try to visit these animals early in the day. If your child has a fear of certain animals avoid that section of the zoo.

Events - Sports/Concerts/Shows

There is always something exciting going on in a big city. Visit the local tourist office or check the Internet for a calendar of events. Take the family to a sporting event, the theatre, the circus, or to a concert to see their favorite pop musician. For travel and tourism information worldwide, contact the Official Government Tourism Information Centers at www.towd.com.

Beginning in February, baseball spring training in Florida is always a thrill for the baseball fan. Your child may even be able to get an autograph from his favorite player. For a spring training schedule visit www.springtrainingconnection.com.

Most stadiums, theatres, and concert halls are wheelchair accessible providing special seating and *ADA* compliant restrooms. Assistant listening devices and sign language may also be available with advance notice.

> ***American Disability Act (ADA)*** – gives civil rights protection to individuals with disabilities

In 2012 the Theatre Development Fund launched a new program, the Autism Theatre Initiative. Selected Broadway shows are performed in a friendly, supportive environment for an audience of families and friends with children who are diagnosed with autism. During the performance loud sounds are reduced and strobe lights are not directed at the audience. A quiet area in the lobby is provided. Visual stories are available several months in advance of the performance on their Web site. For additional information visit the Theatre Development Fund Web site at www.tdf.org.

What to do next?

After completing the Family Interest Planner and reading this chapter, you have an idea of the vacation that will work for your family. In the next chapter, we provide information about special provisions and accessibility for a child with ambulatory, medical, visual, deaf or hard of hearing, and/or special dietary needs.

*I can't change the direction of the wind, but I can adjust
my sails to always reach my destinations.*
– Jimmy Dean

DETERMINE
SPECIAL PROVISIONS REQUIRED
FOR TRAVEL

I n this chapter, we discuss special provisions and accessibility for accommodations, attractions, and modes of transportation for a child with ambulatory, medical, visual, deaf or hard of hearing, and/or special dietary needs.

Answer the questions on the Special Needs Pre-Trip Questionnaire to help identity the special provision required to enable travel for your child. When you have completed the questionnaire, review the needs identified and proceed to the section that addresses those needs. For example, if you identified an ambulatory need for your child on the Special Needs Pre-Trip Questionnaire, you will want to focus your attention on that section of this chapter. Use the information to make final decisions about your travel dreams and special provisions that will need to be part of your vacation planning.

Special Needs Pre-Trip Questionnaire

Ambulatory Needs

1. **Does your child have physical limitations?**
   If yes, describe.

2. **Does your child need special provisions?**
   These may include:
   ☐ Wheelchair accessible room
   ☐ Handgrips in the bathroom
   ☐ Roll-in shower
   ☐ Other

   Describe additional provisions.

Medical Needs

3. **Does your child have significant health issues?**
   These may include:
   ☐ Seizure disorder
   ☐ Diabetes
   ☐ Heart problems
   ☐ Lung problems

   Describe additional health concerns.

4. **Does your child take any medication?** If yes, what medical supplies will you need to bring for your child to take the medication (e.g., syringe)?
   List medications and any related supplies.

5. **Is refrigeration necessary for medications or special foods or beverages?**
   - ☐ Yes
   - ☐ No

Visual Needs

6. **Does your child have a visual impairment?**
   If so, are any special provisions or devices needed?
   - ☐ Braille
   - ☐ Large print menus
   - ☐ Service dog
   - ☐ Cane travel

Describe additional devices or special provisions.

Needs for the Deaf or Hard of Hearing

7. **Is your child deaf or hard of hearing?**
   If so, are any special provisions or devices needed?
   - ☐ Visual alert alarms (smoke, door knock)
   - ☐ VideoPhone or VideoPhone Program
   - ☐ Internet Protocol Program for Relay Calls
   - ☐ Captioned Phone
   - ☐ Amplified Phone
   - ☐ Television and satellite/cable service with built in caption decoders
   - ☐ Alarm clock with light or vibration alert
   - ☐ Real-time captioning
   - ☐ Loop systems
   - ☐ FM or other assistive listening systems

☐ Sign language interpreters or other forms of interpreters
☐ Hearing aid
☐ Service animal

Describe additional devices or special provisions.

Special Dietary Needs

8. **Does your child or anyone else traveling with you have any dietary restrictions? If so, please describe:**
   ☐ Gluten/casein free diets
   ☐ Allergies
   ☐ Kosher
   ☐ Other:

Caregiver Needs

9. **Do you, as the caregiver, have any special transportation needs?**
   If so, describe any special equipment you may need.

10. **Does your child require nursing services on a day-to-day basis?**
   ☐ Yes
   ☐ No

Go to starbritetravel.com to download this form.

Ambulatory Needs

Cruises

- Check the age of the ship. Newer ships tend to have better wheelchair/walker accessibility and medical equipment for children with mobility issues.
- Request a cabin that is near the elevator if your child has difficulty walking long distances or uses a walker.
- Request a wheelchair accessible room, which may include a roll in shower, raised toilet seat, lowered sink, fold-down shower bench, hand-held showerhead, handgrips in bathroom and shower, and lowered closet rods.
- Contact the cruise line at least 60 days in advance to ensure all mobility equipment, accessible transfers, and medical supplies are in place.
- Special Needs at Sea (www.specialneedsatsea.com) and Care Vacation (www.carevacations.com) deliver equipment and supplies directly to the cruise ship. See Appendix 3 for additional information about resources for travel.
- Inquire if doors to deck areas open automatically with the touch of a button.
- Request a van with a lift for transfers.
- Inquire about a hydraulic lift for pools.
- It is recommended that dry cell batteries be used in wheelchairs and mandatory that all mobility devices be stored and recharged in the stateroom.

★ **Tip**

Bring your own extension cord in the event the ship is unable to provide one to charge wheelchair.

Finding the best shore excursions for your family when traveling with a child with special needs takes research and preparation.

> **Tenders** – a small boat that transports passengers from the cruise ship to the shore

Shore excursions might be the most difficult part of cruising for someone with a mobility impairment. Investigate the activity level of the excursion, as well as any equipment you may need. If your child uses a walker or has difficulty walking long distances you may want to choose an excursion with a minimal activity level. Most cruise lines identify wheelchair accessible or slow walker excursions in their brochures. This information can also be found on the cruise line Web site for your specific ship and destination. For safety reasons, choose a shore excursion that has ports of call that directly dock at the pier. Motorized wheelchairs and mobility scooters normally cannot be taken on *tenders*. For a list of ports of call where the cruise ship docks at the pier check with the cruise line.

Before booking an excursion consider the following questions:

- Does your child have difficulty walking long distances?
- Can your child climb up and down the steps of the motor coach?
- Are wheelchair lift vans or motor coaches available at each port of call?
- Is your child able to transfer out of the wheelchair onto the seat of a car?
- Where is the nearest hospital at the port of call?

Accommodations

- Hotels are required by the American Disability Act to provide wheelchair accessible rooms. (www.ada.gov/pubs/ada.htm)
- Wheelchair accessible rooms have wider doors, grips for tubs and toilets, and a roll-in shower. Requests for these rooms need to be made at the time of booking.
- For questions regarding wheelchair accessibility, contact the resort or hotel directly and ask for the general

46

manager or special needs desk. They will be able to answer questions about accessibility and other requests you may have. Be specific, ask:

- Is the path to the pool paved or gravel?
- Are beach wheelchairs available to rent at the hotel or a nearby surf shop?
- Is there access to all areas of the resort for those who use a wheelchair or walker?
- Prior to leaving for vacation, locate an equipment supply store near your hotel in case of equipment breakage.
- When traveling internationally do not plug your wheelchair into the hotel's razor plug. It can only accept 15-watt appliances and will blow a fuse and destroy your equipment. A universal charger is available for wheelchairs and scooters from Soneil (www.soneil.com).

Attractions

- Most zoos, amusement parks, aquariums, and museums are wheelchair accessible. Often *accessible guide maps* with layout routes for wheelchair users are available at the

> *Accessible guide map* – a map that show accessible features of the facility
> *Rough terrain* – irregular surface

customer service desk. These maps will identify areas that may have inclines or *rough terrain*, which may make it difficult for children who have difficulty walking, use a walker or wheelchair.
- Wheelchairs are typically available to rent at guest relations. The numbers of wheelchairs vary from attraction to attraction and are usually available on a first-come-first-serve basis. Call ahead to reserve a wheelchair.
- Elevators and ramps are usually located throughout facilities with access to all floors.

- Interactive hands-on exhibits at museums tend to have counters and tables at an accessible height for wheelchair users.

★ **Tips**

If your child is interested in snorkeling, but has a physical disability that will prevent swimming, an inflatable raft with a window is the way to go. Your child can lie on the raft and use the window to view the underwater world. If possible, purchase one before leaving home or rent at a surf shop or dive store. If you plan to rent, check for availability.

Beach wheelchairs can be rented at most beach vacation destinations. These plastic or aluminum chairs are equipped with mesh seating slings and oversized tires that will not sink into the sand.

Transportation

Air travel

- Prior to air travel, be sure to review *Transportation Security Administration (TSA)* regulations for equipment requirements, dimensions of wheelchairs, medical portable electronic devices, ventilators, respirators or regulations regarding batteries. http://www.tsa.gov/traveler-information/travelers-disabilities-and-medical-conditions

> *Transportation Security Administration (TSA)* – agency responsible for safeguarding U.S. transportation systems and ensuring safety

- If your child requires a wheelchair on the plane, request an "airplane specific wheelchair" when booking to enable him to maneuver the aisles and lavatory.

- When going through security, you will not be separated from your child. If a private screening is required, you escort and remain with your child throughout the entire process. Security officers will not remove your child from his mobility aid (wheelchair or scooter). You are responsible for removing your child from his equipment.
- If your child is unable to walk or stand, the security officer will conduct a pat-down search of your child while he stays in his mobility aid. A visual and physical inspection of the equipment will also be conducted.
- Use gel or foam-filled batteries in your scooter or power chair to avoid the requirement to remove standard acid-filled batteries and pack them in a special container.
- If using a folding wheelchair, request that it be stowed in the on-board coat closet. There is only space for one wheelchair so arrive early. Include a wheelchair information card to help staff if disassembly is required.
- Attach luggage tags with your name, address, phone number, and gate-number on all equipment.
- Passengers with prosthesis can be screened without removing them. The prosthesis can be screened using the *advanced imaging technology machine*, a metal detector, or a thorough pat down. An officer will need to see the prosthetic, which may require lifting your child's clothing. It is not necessary to expose any sensitive areas or remove a belt that holds the prosthesis to the passenger's body. Security officers will also use technology to test the

> ***Advanced imagining technology machine*** - a machine used by TSA to scan passengers for banned metallic and non-metallic objects. This machine creates an image of the passenger. A passenger must stand still for several seconds in the center of the machine with their arms raisedover their heads

prosthesis for traces of explosive material. If a passenger voluntarily removes his prosthesis during screening, it will be screened by x-ray.

> **Bulkhead** –seats that give more room in front of a passenger on an airplane
> **Shuttle vehicle** – a public transport bus service designed to transport people between points – usually from airport to hotel

- Request movable armrests for your child's seat.
- Request *bulkhead* seating to give your child more room.
- Call the airlines ahead to arrange a *shuttle vehicle* to your gate.
- Assistive devices brought onto the airplane by individuals with a disability do not count toward a limit on carry-on items.

Public ground transportation

Most cities have accessible public transportation such as buses, trains, and subways. Visit the Web site of the Department of Transportation for the city you are visiting to verify the accessibility. The majority of buses have lifts. Newer buses have low floors that enable customers to enter via front door ramps. All stations are not wheelchair accessible.

Train and subway stations are often wheelchair accessible. Accessible subway stations and train stations provide:

- Elevators or ramps
- Accessible height station booth-windows and metro card vending machines
- Accessible restrooms
- Telephone accessibility
- Auto gates, an automatic entry, and exit gate
- Ramps, mini-high level platforms, or portable lifts

- Bridge plates are available at all high and mini high-level platforms to bridge the gap between the platform and the train for safe and easy boarding.

Amtrak will provide assistance to passengers with a disability who use a mobility device such as a wheelchair or walker:

- For high platforms, Amtrak will provide assistance crossing the gap between the platform and the train by using a bridge plate.
- For low-level platforms, Amtrak will provide access to the train through the use of station-based mobile lifts.
- For bi-level trains, Amtrak will provide a ramp or station-based mobile lift to provide access to the lower level of the train.

Mobility devices should not exceed 30 inches wide and 48 inches long, and should have a minimum of 2 inches of ground clearance. The weight limit for an occupied wheeled mobility device is 600 pounds. Amtrak permits both manually operated and battery powered wheeled mobility devices that meet these specifications.

Car and van rentals

Rent an accessible van or mini-van for freedom and independence to travel to different locations. Most rental companies offer daily or weekly rates. You can choose a full-size van or a mini-van. See Appendix 3 for accessible van rental companies.

Medical Needs

My daughter, Emma, has spastic quadriplegic cerebral palsy. With the help of Starbrite Kids Program, we chose to stay at the Polynesian Hotel in Disney World. We utilized the monorail; this made getting from park to park so simple. We referred to the comprehensive packet we were given by the Starbrite staff which provided us with personalized visual stories, detailed information about the parks and hotel, contact information and location of first aid buildings as well as handicap accessibility to every ride and attraction. We were also provided with a Guest Assistant pass to enter the rides using a shorter line. Each park gave us full access to their first aid facilities to change Emma and a private room to feed her via g-tube. Due to all of the accommodations that were arranged by the staff at Starbrite, Emma's experiences ranged from flying on the magic carpet ride to going on an African Safari.
--N.C., New Jersey

Cruises

- Newer ships usually have the best medical facilities.
- Inform the disability specialist on the cruise line in advance about your child's medical needs.
- Meet with medical staff once on board to discuss your child's needs.
- Inquire about procedures if a *medical evacuation* is necessary due to an emergency.
- Check if your medical insurance includes cruise medical evacuation.

Medical evacuation – transfers from cruise ship to hospital via helicopter or ground transportation
Trip insurance – insurance that is intended to cover medical expenses and other losses incurred when traveling

- Inquire about vacation *trip insurance* that includes airlift coverage in the event of an emergency.
- Guests requiring continuous ambulatory peritoneal dialysis need to have all solutions and equipment required to perform the dialysis delivered to the ship at least 2 hours before sailing. Dialysis at Sea Cruises specializes in the treatment of hemodialysis care while on-board cruise ships. For additional information visit http://www.dialysisatsea.com/
- Services such as Care Vacation and Special Needs at Sea will deliver all medical supplies or oxygen to the ship. See Appendix 3 for additional information.

Accommodations

- If your child is asthmatic or suffers from other breathing problems, stay at a hotel with air conditioning.
- Depending on your child's needs you may want to choose accommodations and attractions near a hospital.
- Make sure you have the following information before you leave home:
- Location of the nearest hospital to your destination. Information can be found at www.hospitalsworldwide.com.
- Location and contact information for the nearest pharmacy and medical supply company. Contact them before leaving to inquire whether they will deliver to your resort or hotel.
- Location and contact information for an English speaking physician near your destination if you are traveling to a foreign country. You can find a physician who will make hotel visits through the International Association for Medical Assistance for Travelers (telephone 1-716-754-4883 or email www.iamat.org).

Extremely Important Information

Bring extra prescriptions of you child's medication. If you are traveling outside the U.S. the prescription must include the scientific name rather than the brand name of the medication. Some FDA-approved products have the same brand names as the U.S. products, but contain completely different active ingredients. For additional information and a list of "Identical U.S. and Foreign Brand Names Associated With Different Active Ingredients" refer to the FDA Public Health Advisory article, January 2006 at www.fda.gov/drugs.

Attractions

- On the attraction's Web site, preview attraction maps to locate first-aid buildings. If maps are not available, locate the first-aid building upon arrival at the attraction.
- Carry extra water bottles to stay hydrated.
- At arrival, locate shaded quiet spots if your child needs to rest throughout the day.

Transportation

Air travel

- Secure a written statement from your child's physician stating that your child is capable of completing the flight safely without requiring extraordinary medical care.
- Nebulizers are allowed through security checkpoints. It will be screened by x-ray, and passengers are required to remove their Nebulizer from its carrying case (facemasks and tubing may remain in the case). A passenger may provide a clear plastic bag in which to place the Nebulizer during x-ray screening; however, a security officer may need to remove it from the bag to test for traces of explosives.
- Make prior arrangements with airlines when booking a flight if medication requires refrigeration.
- Remain hydrated on flight.

- The *Federal Aviation Administration (FAA)* requires all medical portable electronic devices be marked with manufacture's label.
- Some airlines allow portable manufacturer approved oxygen concentrators on the airplane. Confirm approval by calling the manufacturer. If the airline carrier does not allow personal oxygen concentrators on the airplane request in-flight oxygen. Make your request in advance. You will have to provide a physician's note. An extra fee is usually charged. For more information about airline travel with oxygen contact individual airlines, TSA CARES 1-855-787-2227, or the American Lung Association at 1-800-586-4872 or www.lungusa.org.
- If necessary, obtain a physician's note stating oxygen cannot be disconnected at check-in points at airport.
- Check with the insulin pump manufacturer about whether your child can walk through the metal detector or advanced imaging technology machine with his insulin pump. If the manufacturer does not recommend this, ask a security officer to visually inspect the pump. Visit http://www.tsa.gov/traveler-information/travelers-disabilities-and-medical-conditions for more information.
- If your child has difficulty walking long distances due to medical issues, call the airport or airlines prior to your trip to arrange a shuttle vehicle to your gate.

> *Federal Aviation Administration (FAA)* – agency of the federal government responsible for ensuring the safety of civil aviation

Public ground transportation

- Oxygen is permitted on trains. Inform the reservation agent at least 12 hours prior to traveling that you will be bringing oxygen on-board the train. Oxygen equipment must meet safety requirements. Equipment must be Underwriter's Laboratory (UL) or Factory Mutual (FM) listed, total tanks cannot exceed 120 pounds, and oxygen equipment must be able to operate without a power source for at least 4 hours. Do not rely solely on the electricity from the train to operate your equipment; bring a battery backup power source with you. Contact individual train lines for additional information for local travel or Amtrak at 1-800-USA-RAIL and ask for special service desk.

- Discounts are often available for travelers with disabilities.

★ Tips

For use in the event of an emergency, obtain written medical information about your child's condition prior to your trip.

Upon arrival in a foreign country, obtain the local emergency telephone number.

Carry your child's medical information with you at all times. If he has an extensive medical history a 911 Medical ID provides an easy to use template to upload medical information to a USB flash drive that can connect to any computer. This USB flash drive folds up into a card that can be easily stored in a wallet. Visit www.911medicalid.com or call 1-866-826-0337 for more information.

If your child uses a feeding pump, pack a portable backpack for easy transport. Special backpacks can be purchased through DME (Durable Medical Equipment) www.dmesupplygroup.com.

If your child requires a nurse on vacation, contact the nursing agency you use at home to help locate a nurse at the location you will be visiting.

Visual Needs

Matthew Puvogel, office assistant at the New York City Mayor's Office for People with Disabilities, provided valuable insight and information about individuals with disabilities when traveling. Matthew who is visually impaired stressed

"When going on vacation, it is important to become familiar with your surroundings to minimize anxiety. A parent or caregiver should describe their surroundings to their child with visual impairments by explaining what is occurring in detail, especially when in large crowds." Matthew emphasized, "A visual story, I believe, is a vital tool to ease anxiety when traveling. This should be in audio format or in Braille so the child can follow the information as their parent reads to them." In addition, "When traveling there is a large amount of stimuli and directions that a child must follow. Checklists are helpful listing what steps to expect when entering and maneuvering in an airport or other location."

Cruises

- *Braille*/tactile signage is provided in cabins and throughout the ship.
- Large print, Braille menus, and activity schedules are available.
- An orientation tour of the ship will be provided by the staff upon request to familiarize your child with the public spaces on the ship.

> **Braille** – a formal written language for individuals with visual impairments where raised symbols are used to represent letters and words
> **Stateroom** – a cabin on a ship

- Service dogs are permitted in all public areas on cruise ships. They must be on a leash or harness when out and about the ship. Service dogs may not be left in the *stateroom* unattended. Guests are responsible for providing food for their dog. Refrigeration for dog food is available, but make requests in advance.

Accommodations

- Inform hotel staff that your child has a visual impairment.
- Inform the hotel at booking if your child will be traveling with a service animal. When you arrive at the hotel, locate the guide dog relief area. This is a designated area on the hotel grounds where pets can relieve themselves.
- Request from the hotel reservation desk or management:
  - Auditory safety devices for your room.
  - An orientation tour of the hotel and your room, including fire exits and procedures.
  - A room that provides the easiest route to the lobby, restaurants, and fire exits.
  - Braille or large print hotel information for older children. Inform the hotel ahead of time since Braille information pamphlets and menus may need to be ordered.

★ Tip

Request an additional room pass key so that your older child can gain independence entering the hotel room and your younger child can have fun using hotel keys. Place a small piece of tape on the card running in the same direction as the visual arrow to help with the placing of the card into the door slot.

Attractions

- Some zoos have a handrail that runs the length of the zoo with buttons that deliver special voice messages that describe the physical characteristics and habitat of the animals. Braille messages may also be inscribed on the handrail throughout the zoo.
- When planning to visit national parks, contact the Office of Special Services to inquire if park information is available in large print, Braille, or on audio. Special guides may be available with ample notice.

- Museums are beginning to accommodate those with visual impairments by incorporating other senses into activities to enhance the museum experience.
- Museums may also have:
  - Labels in Braille that identify objects.
  - Audio guides developed by curators about works of art in the museum. Audio guides are free for those with visual impairments.
  - Verbal imaging tours that lead you through the museum by a specially trained museum guide to provide a vividly detailed verbal description of featured pieces, discussing media, texture, style, subject matter, and technique.
  - Touch tours are hands on experiences in which your child can feel selected pieces, such as sculptures and artifacts.

★ **Tip**

Purchase plastic animal figures that your child can hold and touch for a tactile experience when visiting museums, zoos, and aquariums. If possible, use taxidermy animals for the actual tactile experience, the more realistic the better.

Transportation

Air travel

- Notify the airline that you need to be seated with your child due to his visual impairment.
- Advise airport and airline personnel that your child will need important information presented to him orally.
- TSA states that your child is allowed to keep his cane with him in order to move safely through security. An officer will physically inspect your child's cane after he is safely through security.

- When traveling with a service animal, notify the airlines when you book your flight. Airlines must permit service animals with appropriate identification on-board. Your child's service dog can remain with him when proceeding through security.

★ **Tips**

An audible luggage locator is helpful to locate your luggage on the carousel at the airport.

Create an accessible map of the travel plan for your child by gluing string on a map outlining the route. This will help children understand where they are, where they are going and the distanced traveled.

My son, Ivan, is 7 years old and [has] ... [visual impairments]. We have been traveling with Ivan since he was a baby, mostly to visit out-of-state doctors and hospitals, but sometimes for fun, too. Most of the time Ivan loves to explore new places, but other times he can become upset or confused by loud sounds that are unfamiliar to him. We often have to explain what is going on around us, especially in busy places like airports, which can be difficult for us because these are times when we need to pay attention to our bags, tickets, and ID's and have little energy left to stop and describe the environment to Ivan. But we have to remember that explaining everything to Ivan in detail is a necessity for him to stay calm. Describing where he is and what we are doing helps him adjust to his surroundings. We usually divide the job between us: for example, mom may check in the bags and find our gate while dad talks to Ivan and explains to him what is going on or lets him touch objects in the airport. We work as a team to get us where we need to go and keep Ivan involved and happy.
--A.B., Massachusetts

Public ground transportation

- Tactile/Braille signage and maps are often available for bus, train, and subway routes. These can be obtained through the city's transit department.
- Most train or subway ticket machines have Braille instructions.
- Audio and visual information systems are available.

Important Information

A white cane provides your child with tactile cues of what is in front of him. It also lets people know that your child is visually impaired. A cane can be used in any type of environment on vacation. To avoid tripping someone, your child should not use his cane if there is a fire or fire drill. He should fold and carry his cane.

Use "sighted guide" technique with your child. The parent or caregiver will stand next to the child and ½ step in front of him. Child will hold the back of the parent's elbow, or depending on the height of the child, lower on the parent's arm, such as the wrist. It is important that the child's arm be bent in a 90-degree position. The parent will guide the child. The child can also use a cane to receive additional information from the environment while being guided by the parent. Practicing this technique is key. The more comfortable the parent, the better the child feels.

Centers for Independent Living, Vocational Rehabilitation Services, Lighthouses for the Blind, Commission for the Blind and Visually Impaired and other agencies throughout the country offer travel-training programs to teach teenagers and adults with disabilities how to travel safely and independently.

Needs for the Deaf or Hard of Hearing

"Last July our family traveled from our home in Virginia to New Jersey for my mother-in-law's 80th birthday. We decided to make this visit not only a time to spend with family, but also realized that this was the perfect opportunity to visit NYC. My husband and I were a little hesitant at first since our 13 year old daughter, Taylor, has a severe hearing loss. Visiting a busy city at times can be difficult for Taylor due to the extra stimuli and background noises. Trying to lip read can be extremely exhausting and overwhelming for her. My sister-in-law suggested that we call Starbrite Kids, a program that helps parents plan trips for children with special needs. After discussing our plans with the Starbrite Kids staff, we were given suggestions of attractions that provided ASL tours, listening devices, and captioning for the hearing impaired. We visited the American Museum of Natural History, The Metropolitan Museum of Art, and the Sony Wonder Tech Lab. We were even able to see a Broadway Show in ASL! Our visit to NYC was a wonderful experience for the entire family."
--H.S., Virginia

Cruises

- Alert kits are available, including visual-tactile alert systems for travelers who cannot hear knocks at the door, the sound of the emergency alarm, the ringing telephone, alarm clock, or the smoke detector.
- Most ships provide text telephones, amplified telephones, and televisions with built in caption decoders (although programming may not be captioned). Bring or request DVD's or download movies onto a laptop, tablet, or other viewing device if your child likes to watch movies.
- Most cruise ships readily provide a sign language interpreter for ship activities as well as on excursion tours with advance notice. Contact the special needs service

department at individual cruise lines. See Appendix 3 for a list of contacts.

- Other forms of interpreters and real time captioning may be requested by contacting the special needs service department at individual cruise lines.
- Request a ship orientation tour to familiarize your child with the layout of the ship.

Accommodations

- Visual and tactile alerting devices and wake up alarm systems are available upon request at most hotels.
- Visible flashing smoke alarms are available.
- *Telecommunication devices (TTY)* may be available in the hotel room as well as the front desk so those who are deaf or hard of hearing can communicate with the front desk using text messages.
- Televisions are required to have captioning built into them.

> *Telecommunication device (TTY)* – special device that enables an individual who is deaf or hard of hearing to use the telephone to communicate by allowing them to type text

Attractions

- Some museums have installed *hearing loops,* which can be picked up by a tiny receiver built into special hearing aids, and *cochlear implants.* When the receiver is turned on, the hearing

> *Hearing loops* – a thin strand of copper wire radiating electromagnetic signals that can be picked up by a tiny receiver built into special hearing aids and cochlear implants
>
> *Cochlear implants* – electronic hearing devices for people with profound deafness or severe hearing loss who do not benefit from a hearing aid

aid receives only the sounds coming directly from a microphone. This type of technology is successfully used in public places throughout Northern Europe. Many museums in the United States are in the process of installing these loops.

- Sign language interpreters and other access options are usually available at museums, amusement parks, and other facilities with advance notice. Be sure to contact all places where you plan to visit to request interpreters or other access options.
- Movie theatres often offer closed captioned movies and this is becoming widespread. Stage theatres, with advance notice, often provide sign language and other kinds of interpreters as well as captioning.

★ **Tips**

Your child may want to turn down or remove his hearing aids at amusement parks to prevent sensory overload.

Identify captioned movies within 30 miles of your location at www.captionfish.org

---

Transportation

Air travel
- At security:
  - Hearing aids - Your child will not be required to remove hearing aids or cochlear implants during the security screening at the airport. In most cases, hearing aids and cochlear implants will not set off the alarms.
  - Body worn hearing aids and personal listening devices may set off the security scanner. If possible, pack these items in your carry-on bag. Notify the security representative that you have these devices.

- Service animals – Your child and the animal will remain together at all times while going through the security checkpoint.
- Remind security officers to look directly at your child when speaking and to speak slowly. The security officer could also write the information down for your child.
- Inform the flight attendant that your child is deaf or hard of hearing. All safety videos on flights are required to be captioned.
- Airplanes carry safety information in a pamphlet that is stored next to every seat on the airplane.
- Closed captioning television is available at most airports, but is not yet common on airplanes. International flights often have captioned or subtitled options on their viewing menu.

Public ground transportation

- Hearing loops have been installed in several train stations throughout the United States for passengers that use hearing aids. This system allows passengers to listen to the announcements eliminating the background noise that would be detected with a hearing aid.
- Reader boards are visible on some trains and buses showing the next station or stop.
- Train and bus stations may have digital display boards with schedule information.

★ Tip

Pack extra batteries and tubing for your hearing aid. Take a portable dehumidifier, hearing aid blower, or HAL-HEN super Dri-Aid container with you to prevent moisture problems, especially if your destination has a warm, humid climate. Important: Once hearing aids absorb moisture, they are not functional until all moisture evaporates.

Special Dietary Needs

I have two children who suffer from anaphylactic food allergies. Going to restaurants at home and on vacation is always difficult. Hidden ingredients and cross contamination are my biggest concerns. I must always verify the ingredients and preparation methods with the kitchen staff. Sometimes this is difficult. Due to the increase of individuals with food allergies, restaurants and theme parks are making an effort to accommodate children with food allergies. On our recent trip to Disney World my children were able to enjoy ice cream (soy) and waffles for the first time in a restaurant. What a thrill for them!
--N.C., New Jersey

Cruises

- Most cruise lines will accommodate all dietary needs including food allergies, gluten-free, low fat, low sodium, vegetarian, and lactose-free diets. Kosher meals are also available upon request.
- At the time of booking, contact a special needs representative who will make sure the chef has all necessary dietary information.
- Once on-board, arrange a face-to-face meeting with the chef to discuss your child's needs.
- Avoid buffets, as there is a high risk of *cross contamination*.

> *Cross contamination –* when one food comes into contact with another food and their proteins mix

- Inform all staff members of your child's allergies that you will come in contact with on your trip. (i.e. staff at children's program, the chef, your cabin attendant/ steward.

Accommodations

- Contact the hotel beforehand to determine if the hotel restaurant is able to accommodate your child's food allergies/special dietary needs.
- Prior to ordering your food, speak with the hotel chef to ensure he is aware of your child's food allergies/special dietary needs.

Attractions

- Contact the restaurants at the attraction to inquire about accommodating your child's special dietary needs.
- Many attractions do not permit coolers, however, if you elect to pack home prepared foods you should carry a physician's note outlining your child's food allergies.

Transportation

Air travel

- Read the airline's allergy policy on their Web site.
- Notify airlines of food allergies when booking your flight.
- If you are planning to bring a liquid drink on the plane for your child, you will be required to provide a physician's note identifying your child's allergies and the need for the drink.
- Inspect and clean the seat area on the plane to prevent contact reactions.
- Use a sheet specifically made for airplane seats to protect your child from contact with any food residue left on the seat. To purchase airplane sheets visit www.planesheets.com.

> *Epinephrine pen* – a medical device used to deliver a measured dose of epinephrine (adrenaline), most often treatment for acute allergic reaction

- TSA requires that an *Epinephrine pen* be in its original package with the printed label attached. A physician's note or prescription must also accompany this pen.

★ **Tips**

Keep the Epinephrine pen with you at all times in case your child has an allergic reaction. Consider having your child wear identification for serious food allergies.

For information about managing food allergies on vacation visit this comprehensive Web site www.foodallergy.org/section/helpful-information.

Create chef cards describing your child's food allergies by downloading and printing pre-made chef cards for the following food allergies: peanuts, tree nuts, dairy, shellfish, fish, seafood, eggs, wheat, soy and gluten free intolerance from www.allergyfreetable.com/chef-cards.aspx. It is best to print cards on bright colored paper or card stock so it stands out from the other orders. You can also create your own cards.

Pack disposable placemats for tables in restaurants to avoid residue food contact.

Public ground transportation
- Vegan, vegetarian, and Kosher meals are available on most Amtrak trains with 72 hours advance notice.
- Amtrak does not offer meals designated as low fat, low sodium, or low cholesterol or meals that are gluten, wheat, or peanut free. Therefore, you will need to pack your own food for your child.

Travel Tips for All Disabilities

Cruises

- Purchase a portable battery operated Motion Detector Alarm System to use on the doors in your cabin. This is especially important if you are in a cabin with a balcony. This system will sound if a door is opened.
- Contact your airline and cruise line to obtain information about specific documentation needed to travel with a service animal. Airlines and cruise ships require advance notification and some may require special forms to be completed in addition to a letter or prescription. It is recommended by the National Service Animal Registry that your service animal wear a solid color harness or vest, service animal patch, and photo ID clipped to leash or harness. Certain destinations require service animals to have specific vaccinations and documentation.

Accommodations

- To minimize the risk of noise, ask for a room away from the elevators or street. Rooms on the first floor may be a good idea as they allow you to avoid using and waiting for elevators.
- Purchase a portable battery operated Motion Detector Alarm System for doors and windows to be placed in your hotel room. This system will alert you if a door or window is open and may be purchased at Radio Shack.
- If you are concerned your child may roll out of the bed in your hotel room, request a bed rail.

Attractions

- To obtain a Guest Assistance Card at theme parks, a physician's note is required stating your child's disability and special provisions.
- A free lifetime access pass for national parks is available to U.S. citizens or permanent residents of the U.S. that have been medically determined to have a permanent disability.

For more information visit http://www.nps.gov/findapark/passes.htm.

- Children with sensory issues may benefit from using earplugs, noise cancelling headphones, and sunglasses.
- When you arrive at an amusement park, locate a quiet, safe place to go if your child becomes over stimulated or lost. See Safety in Chapter 3.

Transportation

Airport

- To help navigate the airport, including security, a TSA representative will meet your family at the airport if requested. Contact TSA at your departing airport at least 72 hours ahead of travel to coordinate checkpoint support with a TSA Customer Service Manager. On the day of your flight, a TSA representative will meet your family at the entrance of the airport and accompany you every step of the way until boarding.
- Travelers may call TSA Cares (1-855-787-2227) a helpline number designed to assist travelers with disabilities and medical conditions.
- Some airports have fun activities for your child while waiting. You can find a list of these airports and activities at www.cheapflights.com/travel/kids-airport-diversion-guide/.

Airplane

- Keeping a child in an airplane seat is always a concern. Children can remove the seat buckle easily. If your child is too large to fit into a car seat, purchase a FAA certified Child Aviation Restraint System (CARES) manufactured by AmSafe. (www.amsafe.com). CARES is a safety harness designed specifically for airplanes. This device hooks onto the airplane seat and provides the same level of safety as a car seat and weighs one pound.

- Request bulkhead seating on airplanes to give your child more room. Make this request when
- booking.

Train

- Amtrak provides a 15% discount on fares for individuals with disabilities as well as one travel companion. You must provide written documentation of your disability at the ticket counter and when boarding the train. Policies may change. For up to date information contact Amtrak at www.Amtrak.com, 1-800-872-7245 or TTY 1-800-523-6590.
- Accessibility guide is available in alternate formats including Braille, large print, audiotape, and diskette. Call 1-800-USA-RAIL/TTY 1-800-523-6590.

What to do next?

By now you and your family have decided where you would like to go on vacation and determined what special provisions need to be put in place prior to travel. You have researched the destinations and inquired if the accommodations and attractions provide accessibility and special provisions to meet the needs of your family. If you as the caregiver require special provision, be sure to address your needs at this time.

Now you can begin to prepare your child for vacation by identifying your child's travel concerns and applying intervention strategies outlined in the next chapter.

Questions and Answers

Q. My daughter has a physical disability and uses a wheelchair. We are flying to Florida this summer. Is there a charge to check her wheelchair at the gate?

A. Most airlines do not charge a fee to check a wheelchair. However, we advise you to call the airlines directly prior to leaving for your trip.

Q. My daughter is hard of hearing. Are there any museums in the New York City area that are equipped with hearing loops?

A. Yes, the Metropolitan Museum of Art and the Museum of Modern Art are equipped with hearing loops.

Q. My son is visually impaired and he would like to see a movie in the theatre. Are there any movie theatres that provide audio descriptions?

A. The Audio Description Project, an initiative of the American Council of the Blind, provides audio description for movies in theatres throughout the country. Audio description is a voice narration that describes the visual elements of a movie. Request an audio description headset at the ticket counter. To locate a theatre that provides audio description services visit www.captionfish.com.

Q. My child has cerebral palsy and is confined to a wheelchair. Are there any amusement parks that have wheelchair accessible rides?

A. Yes, Morgan's Wonderland in San Antonio, Texas is the first ultra-accessible family fun park, offering 30 traditional, adaptive, and wheelchair swings along with many other rides and activities. Morgan's Wonderland vision is to create an atmosphere of inclusion for those with and without disabilities to play and enjoy life together.

Q. My son is on the autism spectrum. We are spending the weekend in NYC and would like to take him to see a Broadway Show. Loud noises and bright lights bother him. Are there any programs that accommodate the needs of children with autism?

A. You are in luck. In 2012 the Theatre Development Fund launched a new program, the Autism Theatre Initiative. Selected Broadway shows are performed in a friendly, supportive environment for an audience of families and friends with children who are diagnosed with autism. During the performance loud sounds are reduced and strobe lights are not directed at the audience. There is also a quiet area in the lobby. Social Stories are also available on the Web site several months in advance of the performance.

Q. My child is quadriplegic and confined to a wheelchair. She is also on a feeding tube. We plan on traveling this year. Do I need to pack all of her supplies such as formula, diapers, and feeding tube equipment?

A. No, you do not need to pack all of her supplies. Throughout the country there are many surgical supply stores where you can purchase supplies. Many will deliver supplies directly to your hotel. Contact a travel consultant that specializes in travel for special needs or check on-line to locate a supply store.

Q. Our family is going to Hawaii on vacation and staying at a hotel on the beach. My child has a physical disability and uses a wheelchair. What equipment is available for him to enjoy the beach?

A. Many beach vacation spots have beach wheelchairs available. The chairs are equipped with mesh seating slings, and oversized tires so they can traverse the sand. Surf shops, lifeguards, or the hotel itself will be able to help you. Be careful near the water, as these chairs tend to float.

Q. My daughter has type 1 Diabetes and is on insulin. We will be crossing time zones when we travel. At home, my daughter is on a strict schedule with her injections. How can we adhere to her schedule as we cross time zones?

A. The first thing you need to do is speak with your daughter's physician and explain the situation. Her physician will be able to help in planning the time of the injections. Keep your watch on your home time zone until you arrive at your final destination. This will help you keep track of meals and shots throughout the transportation part of the trip.

Q. My son is on the autism spectrum. Are there any hotels or resorts that have special provisions for children with autism?

A. Yes, hotels are realizing that children with autism have special needs they need to handle. Hotels such as Tradewinds Island Resort in St. Petersburg, Florida and Wyndham Hotel in Tampa Bay, Florida have been approved by the Center for Autism and Related Disabilities as autism friendly hotels. These hotels provide safety kits, sensory activities, gluten-free menus, dimming lights, and allergy free cleaning products. All staff members have been trained by the Center for Autism and Related Disabilities.

Tomorrow's victory is today's practice.
-- Chris Bradford

DRY RUN
PRE-TRAVEL REHEARSAL

In this chapter we will look at concerns you may have about traveling with your child and strategies to prepare your child for vacation. Travel itself presents experiences that require learning new behaviors and interacting with unfamiliar people. For example, your child may be navigating the airport and flying in an airplane for the first time. Other new experiences include riding a subway, sleeping in a different bed, and eating at new restaurants. Through all of this, your child must also practice safe behavior. All of these aspects of travel are wonderfully exciting, but may also pose challenges for some children.

In our discussions with parents, their children's challenging behavior is the primary reason they avoid traveling as a family. Parents stated that their children had difficulty coping with the demands and stresses of travel. Do you have concerns about your child:

- Getting ready for the trip?
- Traveling to your destination?
- Participating in the different activities and attractions you have planned while traveling?
- Trying new activities while traveling?
- Handling all the changes that occur while traveling?
- Engaging in challenging behavior?
- Communicating and interacting with unfamiliar people while on vacation?
- Being safe while traveling?

If you answered yes to any of these questions, you are not alone. Many parents share these common concerns. The goal of this chapter is to address these concerns so your child and your family can enjoy taking a family vacation.

This chapter is titled Dry Run because much of what you do to get your child ready for travel will involve practice and preparation before travel. You will want to begin to address each travel concern well before you leave for vacation. We often practice without even thinking about it; we practice the lines of a poem for school, we recite in the mirror what we want to say to someone, and we practice a skill before we perform it in public.

Practice is the best master.
-- Latin Proverb

The Starbrite Kids Three Steps will help you identify potential travel concerns, develop strategies to address those concerns, and prepare your child for travel by:

- Creating excitement and anticipation for the trip
- Familiarizing your child with the upcoming trip
- Relieving anxiety your child may feel about traveling
- Teaching your child important travel skills

Starbrite Kids Three Steps to Prepare for Travel

Step One	**Discuss the Trip with Your Child**
Step Two	**Identify Travel Concerns**
Step Three	**Use Strategies to Address Travel Concerns**

To illustrate preparing for travel, let's apply our Starbrite Kids Three Steps to Ms. P. and her son John.

> ## John's Family Vacation
>
> John is an 8 year old child with an autism spectrum disorder. Ms. P. is planning a vacation, but has concerns about her son's ability to handle traveling.
>
> *I really want to take John on vacation with our family, however, due to his inability to handle changes, I am afraid he will become very anxious and act out. Traveling may be just too much for all of us. I wish I knew what to do.*
> *– Ms. P., Pennsylvania*

Step One - Discuss the Trip with Your Child

First, discuss the trip with your child. This will help you identify concerns that will need to be addressed to prepare your child for a successful trip. The planning you did in Chapter 1 may also help you to identify concerns. Pick a quiet time when you and your child can sit together to talk about the trip. Discuss:

- Where you will go
- When you will travel
- How you will travel
- What you will see
- With whom you will travel
- People you may meet
- What behaviors are expected

Remember no detail is too small. Use brochures, maps, videos, magazines, and the Internet to give your child an idea of what to expect. How familiar is your child with the different planned activities? Does he know what he will do and see at the various activities? For example, if you are going to the aquarium and your child has never been to one, you may want to provide some information of what he may see when he gets there. Many aquariums in the United States provide a preview of the animals and fish you will see at their facility, as well as puzzles, games, and coloring activities on their Web site. Other attractions you might visit may have similar information available on their Web sites.

If your child asks you to explain something, provide as many details as you can that are appropriate for your child's age. For example, when you show your child a picture of the hotel room, he may ask, "Who will be in my room?" "Can I bring my teddy bear?" "Where will you sleep?" Respond to your child with details to answer his questions.

Listen to and observe your child's reactions and emotions when you discuss the details of the vacation. Which attractions seem to interest or excite your child? Look for signs of distress, such as your child covering his eyes and ears, withdrawing, avoiding the conversation, looking away, engaging in self-stimulatory behaviors, or crying. Discuss what is upsetting him and brainstorm together what to do to address the problem. Ask your child what he should do when presented with a problem traveling. For example, if your child has difficulty waiting to be served in a restaurant, ask him what behaviors are appropriate and inappropriate when required to wait.

Reflect on your child's reactions during the planning stage in Chapter 1 and on other trips or outings. Remember how your child reacted when faced with challenging situations in the past. This may have been on a previous vacation or a community outing such as shopping or dining out.

Ask others to think of any situations that might be problematic for your child when taking a vacation. Teachers, caregivers, and siblings may come up with other concerns.

Remember: If you are planning many activities and your child has difficulties *transitioning*, it may be best to discuss one part of the trip or one activity at a time.

Start out with something you know your child will love. Take it slow; your child may need time to process the plans. Let your child be

> *Transitioning* – a change from one activity to another

your guide. You might discuss the trip a few times with your child so you have an opportunity to discuss all the various aspects of the trip (e.g., discuss transportation, hotel, and activities at different times) to see what your child gets excited about and what concerns him. Give your child time to think and reflect about what was discussed.

Step One - Ms. P. Discusses the Trip with John

Ms. P. picks a quiet time to discuss their trip to Florida. She shows John a picture of the aquarium they will be visiting on vacation. John becomes excited when looking at pictures of the fish. John loves to watch the fish in the tank at his aunt's house and can identify many of the different species. Ms. P. then shows John pictures of the hotel and the airplane; she discusses how they will drive to the airport, get on a plane, and then drive to a hotel in Florida. John becomes visibly upset. He begins covering his ears and rocking. Due to John's difficulty with transitions, his reaction did not come as a surprise to Ms. P.

Knowing John's difficulties with transitioning, Ms. P. decides to change the topic of conversation and ask John if he would like to pick something special to do on their flight to Florida. This diverts his attention to a more pleasant part of the vacation. Ms. P. will continue the conversation about the hotel and airport at another time. Ms. P. reminds John about visiting the aquarium so that she ends the discussion on a positive note.

Step Two – Identify Travel Concerns

Now that you have discussed the trip with your child, and have identified travel concerns that need to be addressed, check off the concerns on the Travel Concern Checklist. The Checklist is comprised of common concerns parents have shared with us, grouped into some of the major aspects of traveling. If one of your specific travel concerns is not listed, add it to the list. Some of the strategies we discuss in Step Three may be modified to address that travel concern.

Step Two – Ms. P. Identifies Travel Concerns

Ms. P. reviews the Travel Concern Checklist and determines that she has several concerns for John. Her primary concern is "transitioning from one activity to another" as it causes the most disruption. She is now ready to move to Step Three.

Travel Concern Checklist

Getting Ready for Vacation
- ☐ Vacation anticipation
- ☐ Active involvement in vacation preparation
- ☐ _____

Transportation
- ☐ Going through airport security
- ☐ Flying on an airplane
- ☐ _____

Vacation Expectations
- ☐ Riding in an elevator
- ☐ Sleeping in a different bed
- ☐ Transitioning from one activity to another
- ☐ Overstimulation at attractions
- ☐ Waiting
- ☐ Eating at restaurants and etiquette
- ☐ Following morning and evening routine
- ☐ _____

Interacting with Others
- ☐ Conversing with different people
- ☐ Meeting unfamiliar relatives
- ☐ Sharing with peers on vacation
- ☐ _____

Staying Safe
☐ Safety
☐ _____

Step Three – Use Strategies to Address Travel Concerns

Now that you have identified your travel concerns in Step Two, it is time to use strategies to address each concern to help prepare your child.

There are many evidence-based intervention strategies to consider in addressing the needs of children when traveling. The strategies we chose have an evidence-base to change behavior and/or teach new skills to children with a variety of disabilities. The strategies have not necessarily been examined in travel situations, but could be applied to such situations. Some strategies have more evidence for use with children with a particular disability, but may be applied to a child with any disability in a travel-related situation. Some of the research associated with each strategy can be found in Appendix 4.

The chart below lists common travel concerns. For each concern, there are a number of potential intervention strategies; we chose to illustrate one strategy to help you address each concern and prepare your child before traveling. You might choose to use a different strategy than the one we discussed, drawing on the material presented throughout the chapter to adapt a strategy to a different concern. For handy reference, we provided a list of concerns and strategies along with page numbers on which each is discussed.

Common Travel Concerns	Strategy	Page
Getting Ready for Vacation		89
Vacation anticipation	Countdown Calendar	89
Active involvement in vacation preparation	Choice Making	94
Transportation		101
Going through airport security	Story	101
Flying on an airplane	Story	109
Vacation Expectations		115
Riding on an elevator	Model and Practice	115
Sleeping in a different bed	Model and Practice	118
Transitioning from one activity to another	Schedule	122
Overstimulation at attractions	Relaxation Techniques	127
Waiting	W.A.I.T Box	133
Eating at restaurants (etiquette)	Video Modeling	136
Following morning/evening routine	Mini Schedule	142

Common Travel Concerns	Strategy	Page
Interacting with Others		145
Conversing with different people	Visual Script	146
Meeting unfamiliar relative	Scrapbook	151
Sharing with peers on vacation	Cartoon	154
Staying Safe		157
Safety rules	Illustrated Scenarios, Interactive Activities	158

Step Three – Ms. P. Uses a Schedule to Address Transitioning

Ms. P. uses a schedule to address *transitioning from one activity to another* when traveling. The schedule will be an outline of the transitions John will make throughout the day. A small spiral notebook will be used so John can keep it in his pocket for easy reference. This will help him understand what to expect, aid with predictability, and reduce anxiety. John reads well, so Ms. P. decides to write each activity for his schedule using a short phrase.

Since John has never used a schedule, Ms. P. and John create and practice using schedules at home prior to going on vacation. Here is an example of John's schedule for a typical school day:

- [ ] Eat breakfast at home with my family
- [ ] Get ready for school
- [ ] Take the bus to school
- [ ] Spend the morning in my classroom doing my schoolwork
- [ ] Lunch in the cafeteria
- [ ] Play on the playground
- [ ] Go back to my classroom
- [ ] Pack backpack for dismissal
- [ ] Take the bus home
- [ ] Do homework
- [ ] Eat dinner
- [ ] Follow daily bedtime routine
- [ ] An extra bedtime story for successfully following the schedule

Ms. P. also talks to John about their trip and how they might use a schedule while on vacation. She and John make a list of things they might do one day of their trip; they prepare a schedule for the first day when they leave for the airport. Ms. P. will includes all transitions John will be required to make throughout the day.

What to do on vacation

Each morning, Ms. P. and John begin their day by preparing a schedule. Ms. P. reflects on her discussion with John in Step One about the upcoming trip. During their discussion, John expressed excitement about visiting the aquarium; therefore, visiting the aquarium is included as one of the day's activities (other activities that John expressed an interest in will be included on other days).

Ms. P. balances John's day by including a rest period as well as a familiar activity, going to the playground. To limit the number of transitions, she chooses to eat breakfast in the hotel and eat lunch at the aquarium. She gives John two choices for dinner; he chooses to eat at a local pizzeria. John and his mother discuss expected behaviors at the aquarium, lunch, and during transitions. Ms. P. identifies reinforcers for appropriate transitions throughout the day. A reinforcer is a reward given to maintain or increase the future likelihood of that behavior. Ms. P. tells John that he can have a special ice cream treat after lunch if he leaves the aquarium after a 10 minute warning without crying. After a smooth transition back to the hotel room in the evening and getting ready for bed, Ms. P. gives John extra time to read before going to bed as a reinforcer.

Example of John's schedule on vacation -

- ☐ Eat breakfast in the hotel restaurant with my family
- ☐ Drive to the aquarium
- ☐ Visit the aquarium and watch the fish
- ☐ Eat lunch in the café at the aquarium – special treat!
- ☐ Go back to our hotel room and rest
- ☐ Walk to the playground
- ☐ Play at the playground
- ☐ Walk to the hotel
- ☐ Eat dinner at the pizzeria across the street
- ☐ Walk back to our hotel room and get ready for bed
- ☐ Follow bedtime routine
- ☐ Receive extra time to read

You are likely to have more than one concern about your child traveling. If so, you will need to prioritize what you want to work on first by asking yourself, "What is the most important concern that needs to be addressed before going away?" Prioritize the most important concerns that you will need to address and use strategies to address those concerns to prepare your child for traveling.

There may be some concerns for which you decide to make alternate arrangements, rather than use the strategies in this chapter. For example, if you know your child is fearful of elevators, you might secure a room on the first floor; if your child has a difficult time at sit down restaurants (waiting or eating), you might plan to eat at a fast food chain, order room service, call ahead for reservations, or order your food ahead of time. You can then focus preparing for the most significant concerns.

In the next section, you will learn about strategies to address each of the common travel concerns. We will walk you through each strategy step by step with ideas about what to do before vacation, on vacation, as well as what to do after vacation.

The strategies in the Dry Run section can be used for children with different types of disabilities. The activities can be formatted in Braille, recorded to audio, or enlarged on paper or a computer screen for children who have visual impairments. For children who are deaf or hard of hearing, any of the activities using audio can be communicated in sign language, text, or with pictures.

For each common concern we:
- Describe the travel concern
- Identify and define one intervention strategy
- Discuss why that strategy might be useful
- Provide steps to use the strategy
- Provide an activity that uses the strategy to practice before vacation
- Discuss how to use the strategy while on vacation (and sometimes after vacation as well)

Getting Ready for Vacation

Getting ready to travel can be exciting and fun, but also may be overwhelming. There are ways to help your child understand when his vacation will happen and get him involved in the preparation process so that getting ready for vacation is a positive experience for all.

Travel Concern - Vacation Anticipation
Intervention Strategy - Countdown Calendar

Planning and preparation take time; many children have difficulty understanding the concept of time. Your child will be more comfortable and excited about the trip if he knows what to expect in the weeks and months leading up to your vacation. A **countdown calendar** will provide him with a visual support to help prepare for travel.

What is a countdown calendar?
A countdown calendar is a way to record the occurrence of special events. The calendar should be readily accessible and visible. The calendar should also be checked regularly to monitor the passage of time until the special event.

Why use a countdown calendar to help with anticipating a vacation?

A calendar provides the perfect tool for your child to track the days and weeks before vacation. A calendar provides predictability, promotes independence, and helps reduce anxiety by giving your child a tool to monitor upcoming travel. Calendars are an easy way to present the abstract concepts of sequence and time in a concrete form. Your child can record events leading up to the trip, make any changes that may need to be made before traveling, and even special activities while traveling.

How to use a countdown calendar
1. Obtain a calendar.
2. Determine how your child will record information on the calendar.
3. Discuss the function of a calendar with your child.
4. Record events on the calendar.
5. Check the calendar regularly.

What to do before vacation
1. Obtain a calendar with your child. Hang the calendar in an easy to reach area. This could be a large wall calendar or a small datebook. Calendars can be purchased or printed from the Internet. Calendars can also be created on your child's computer or phone.
2. Determine how your child will record information on the calendar. Will he use written words, stickers, symbols, or pictures?
   - If your child is a non-reader, you may want to use pictures to identify special events on his calendar. Printing clipart off the Internet can be a great solution since you can modify the size of the picture to fit his calendar. Make sure your child will be able to associate the picture with the event.
   - Use images that are simple, clear, and uncluttered.

- If your child can draw, have him draw a picture to indicate the event (e.g., draw a dog for the day your dog will go to the kennel; an airplane for the day he will fly).
- If your child can write, he may write in the events; you can provide a model for him to copy if he cannot spell the words on his own.
- If your child can read, but not readily write, you can write out the events on small pieces of paper for him to affix to the calendar on the appropriate day.

3. Discuss the use of a calendar to mark special events such as birthdays, school activities, upcoming trips, doctor, and dentist appointments. Discuss how to use a calendar as a reminder of what to do on a specific day. This reminder can also help you and your child prepare ahead of time for the days' activities (e.g., knowing what to wear the day he goes to karate class). You might model for your child how you use your own calendar. For example, put a special event such as your child's upcoming birthday on your calendar. Then in the weeks prior note activities you have to do to prepare for the birthday party (e.g., send out invitations, order the cake, purchase balloons).

4. Record with your child events on your child's countdown calendar including the vacation. Put on the calendar important and fun dates prior to vacation such as taking your passport picture, shopping for new clothes, renting skis, packing suitcases, preparing the fun bag, bringing the dog to the kennel, and printing out boarding passes for the flight. Put several events on the calendar so your child will have several opportunities to check the calendar and countdown the days until an event.

5. Check the calendar regularly with your child (e.g., every morning). Your child can:
   - Identify if there is an important event that day.
   - Cross off the day on the calendar so he can visually see the approach of the vacation.

- Count the days left until he leaves for vacation. Your child can also record this information somewhere on or near the calendar.

★ Tips

Pack a fun bag to take on vacation. Fill the bag with items you know your child will love, let him choose some of the items, and surprise him with something special "when the going gets rough."

Get your child involved with the planning of the attractions you will visit on vacation. Your child can select a "kid's choice" activity or meal. Mark your child's choice on the calendar.

Juanita is a 9 year old girl with a visual impairment. Juanita is very excited about the upcoming vacation asking her mother everyday if this is the day they are leaving. She is also worried that she will not have enough time to go shopping for new clothes for the trip. Juanita's mom decides to use a countdown calendar to help with her vacation anticipation. Since Juanita has a visual impairment her mother uses large font, contrasting colors, and outlines the numbers using a hot glue gun to provide a tactile experience. She also hangs the calendar in an area of her house that has minimal glare.

What to do on vacation

- Bring your calendar on vacation. If you used a big wall calendar, create a pocket sized one for travel. You might also consider putting the calendar on a phone or computer. If you continue to use the calendar during travel, it may help with the transition of going home and can even be used as part of a visual schedule to help with transitions during the trip. (Transitioning will be discussed later in this chapter).

- Your child can also record what he did each day of his trip on the calendar. This may be used to help your child share with others upon returning home, providing him with a visual reminder of his vacation. He can also use a portable audio recorder, digital recording pen, or tablet.

Travel Concern - Active Involvement in Vacation Preparation
Intervention Strategy - Choice Making

Traveling involves lots of planning and preparation, much of which you have begun in Chapters 1 and 2 with your child. You can continue to involve your child in preparing for vacation. Doing so allows your child some control over the trip and may decrease challenging behavior and increase participation. **Choice making** is a strategy to support your child's involvement in certain decisions about the trip. We will illustrate choice making with packing for vacation, but you could apply choice making to final decisions about what attractions to visit and when, restaurants to try, foods to eat, and leisure activities.

What is choice making?
Choice making is a positive behavioral strategy that occurs when a person is given two or more options from which to choose. Choice making promotes independence and decision making and gives children a sense of control. Providing opportunities to make choices is an appropriate strategy to use with children of all ages. The types of choices will need to be modified to suit children of different ages.

Why use choice making to help with vacation preparation?
We chose choice making for this situation because when you give your child choices, you give him a sense of control, which in turn promotes compliance and positive behavior. Choice making is an effective strategy to increase children's participation.

How to use choice making
1. Identify desired behavior.
2. Provide your child with information about the trip to help your child make good choices.
3. Give your child 2-3 choices.
4. Direct your child to choose.
5. Reinforce appropriate behavior.

Important
Introduce choices about many aspects of your trip. Provide your child with choices about what treats, toys, games, or other activities your child would like to put in his fun bag for travel. Give him a limited number of choices, making sure the objects are small enough to fit in a backpack and appropriate for travel. For example, a choice between two hand held video games would be appropriate options, but a choice between a 50 piece Lego-set and a box of trains would not be. In the latter, both choices are not appropriate for taking on vacation.

What to do before vacation

1. Identify desired behavior - ***Active involvement in vacation preparation by making choices about packing***
2. Provide your child with information about the trip (e.g. weather, type of activities) to help your child make good choices. Use the photos and information from when you discussed the trip with your child in Step One at the beginning of the chapter.
3. Give your child 2-3 choices of what clothes to pack for vacation. Pick options that are appropriate and acceptable to you. For example, put three shirts on your child's bed and have him choose two. His cognitive and developmental level will determine the number of options you give.
4. Direct your child to choose and repeat with additional choices about the rest of the clothes (and toys) to pack.
5. Reinforce your child's choices by honoring them with praise. Repeat providing choices until you have packed everything necessary for vacation. See Packing Checklist in Chapter 4 to help you identify everything you will need.

Jack is a 13 year old boy who exhibits oppositional defiant behaviors. When his parents approached him with the news about the upcoming vacation he responded, "I don't want to go on any stupid vacation." At that point Jack's parents had two choices, cancel the trip or get Jack involved in planning the vacation. They chose the latter. Jack's parents included him in the planning stages of the trip, offering him acceptable choices about attractions to visit on vacation as well as packing. This enabled Jack to have some control, giving him a sense of independence. On vacation Jack's parents will continue to provide Jack choices about where to have meals and what to do during free time.

What to do on vacation

- Give your child choices about activities over which he can exert control. For example, provide him with choices on what clothes to wear, what and where to eat, and leisure activities. The following are examples of giving choices:

- **Clothing -** "Kate, we are going to the zoo today. Two outfits are on your bed, you can choose whichever one you want to wear today."
- **Food** - "Kate, we are eating in our room tonight, would you like pizza or pasta for dinner?"
- **Leisure activities - "**Kate, we have some time before dinner, would you like to stop at the park or go back to the hotel room to read a book?"

- Remember to honor your child's choice. You may also use a Behavior Specific Praise Statement such as, "Nice job deciding on what to wear, Kate" or, "Pizza is a good choice, thank you, Kate." See tip box, Reinforce Desired Behavior, for more information about Behavior Specific Praise Statements.

Reinforce Desired Behavior

Throughout our Three Step process, reinforce your child's appropriate behavior.

Identify Reinforcers

First, you need to identify objects or activities that can serve as reinforcers. What motivates your child? Think about your child's interests and the activities he engages in when given the opportunity to choose what to do. Your child may enjoy playing with stickers, or extra computer time; your child may seek attention, such as going out to lunch with you. Make a list of preferred items and activities that you could use as reinforcers.

Identify Desired Behavior

Once you decide on what may serve as a reinforcer, you need to identify the behavior your child must engage in to obtain the reinforcer. Be clear and specific about what behavior needs to occur to obtain the reinforcer. For example, if you want to improve restaurant behavior, you might identify sitting in the seat at the restaurant quietly and using restaurant manners as the desired behaviors. If your child sits in his seat quietly for the entire meal and uses manners, he may have dessert after dinner.

Decide on Frequency

Decide when and how often you will provide a reinforcer. Will you provide a small reinforcer every few minutes your child engages in a desired behavior or not until the end of the activity? Will you provide a reinforcer after your child completes each step of an activity (e.g., each step of going through security at the airport)? For example, to improve restaurant behavior, dessert provided after dinner requires your child to engage in the desired mealtime behavior for the entire meal to earn that reinforcer. Alternatively, you could decide to provide praise or stickers more frequently throughout the meal when your child engages in the desired behavior.

Provide Reinforcers

Reinforcers should be given immediately following a desired behavior. Mix and vary reinforcers to ensure the items continue to function as reinforcers.

Types of Reinforcers

Tangible

- Toys
- Special treats
- Watching a movie/television show
- Games, extra computer time

Social

- Hugs
- Behavior Specific Praise Statements
- High fives
- Thumbs up
- A pat on the shoulder
- A compliment
- A smile
- A nod
- Special time with a parent (e.g., going to a special store, the playground, or reading an extra story at bed time)

Behavior Specific Praise Statements (BSPS) are positive statements intended to reinforce desired behavior. A BSPS is a type of verbal praise that specifically describes/identifies the behavior you intend to praise. A BSPS can be given with other reinforcers (e.g., toys, treats) and are effective for any age or ability level (Sutherland, Wehby, & Copeland, 2000). A BSPS can be used anytime on vacation when you want to reinforce behavior.

How to give a BSPS:
- Make a pleasant facial expression.
- Specifically describe your child's positive behavior.
- Include your child's name in the statement.
- Use praise terms such as great job, you did it, way to go, nice job, well done, awesome job, fantastic, amazing, wonderful.
- Give praise immediately.
- Make sure praise is appropriate to your child's language level so your child understands what behavior you are complimenting.
- Vary praise terms.
- Remember you are looking for what your child did right.

Your child's name + praise term + description of positive behavior=
Behavior Specific Praise Statement
"Michelle, good job waiting in line to be seated."

A **Token System** is another strategy to reinforce desired behavior in which a child receives a token for engaging in a desired behavior that he then cashes in for a backup reinforcer at a later time. For example, Shana has difficulty waiting. To address waiting, her mother is going to provide Shana with a poker chip whenever she successfully waits (e.g., waits for her meal at a restaurant, waits in line for a ride at the amusement park). Each time Shana waits quietly, without yelling at her parents or falling to the ground, she will receive a token. At the end of the day, Shana will count her chips. Because there will be lots of waiting opportunities, Shana's mother knows they will not all go smoothly. She sets a criterion number of tokens that Shana must earn by the end of the day allowing for two instances when Shana did not appropriately wait and did not earn a token. If Shana has the required amount of tokens she will cash them in for a reinforcer that has been previously decided by Shana and her mother.

How to use a token system
- Identify desired behavior.
- Select an item to be used as a token. It could be stars or checks on a chart, stickers, poker chips, or a punch hole on a card. While traveling, make it as easy as possible and portable.
- Set the value of the token and time interval for which the token will be given. That is, what behavior does the child need to engage in to earn a token? Are tokens provided after each instance of the desired behavior or after the child engages in the behavior for an amount of time (e.g., sitting in a restaurant for 5 minutes). In Shana's case, each time she successfully waited, she earned a token.
- Determine how many tokens your child will need to receive the backup reinforcer.
- Decide on the reinforcer. Involve your child in identifying a reinforcer.
- Once child earns the required tokens, provide him with the reinforcer. If he does not earn the reinforcer, calmly state why he did not meet criteria and plan to begin the token system again the next time your child needs to engage in the desired behavior.

Transportation

Transportation is part of your child's everyday life, traveling to school, going on class trips, or around the community. When going on vacation your child may need to use modes of transportation such as airplanes, trains, or subways that are unfamiliar to him. Transportation frequently involves needing to wait, something that may be difficult for your child. Refer to the section on waiting later in this chapter for additional strategies.

Travel Concern - Going Through Airport Security
Intervention Strategy - Story

Going through airport security can be anxiety inducing for adults –imagine the experience for a child. For a child with special needs, going through security at an airport can also be particularly challenging. The security machines are big and strange. There are lots of people rushing around in tight spaces with bright lights and lots of sounds. There is lots of waiting in long lines. Security guards may need to touch passengers (pat downs). Bags have to be placed in just the right way to proceed through the scanners.

If your child has a visual impairment or is deaf or hard of hearing, not being able to see or hear the activities when going through airport security may result in greater fear or anxiety. In this case, it is extremely important to help your child prepare ahead of time and then be sure to describe the process as it is happening. Make sure you alert the airport security officer that your child has a visual impairment or deaf or hard of hearing. For children who are hard of hearing, remind the security officer to look directly at your child, speak slowly, and in a normal tone voice when he gives instructions about how to proceed through security. For a child with a visual impairment explain to the security officer that all information has to be given orally, that your child will not be able to see hand gestures (e.g., a security officer waving his hand to signify that your child should proceed through security).

One way to begin to prepare your child for this new experience and help him practice what to do is to use a **story** about going through airport security.

What is a story?

A story provides a description of situations including what might be expected of your child and their feelings in the situation. Carol Gray's Social Stories™ is a well-known example of a story-based strategy.

Why use a story to help your child with transportation concerns?

Stories are excellent tools to use to familiarize your child with different activities he may encounter while traveling. Stories will provide your child with information about what will happen and what behaviors he is expected to engage in while traveling. Stories may help alleviate some of your child's worry about transportation. Include pictures or audio in the story to help your child understand all the information about these new situations.

How to use a story
1. Identify desired behavior.
2. Create the story.
3. Review and discuss the story with your child.
4. Practice the skill discussed in the story at home before to your trip.
5. Reinforce the behaviors you want to encourage.

These steps are partially based on Carol Gray's Social Stories™ (Gray & Garand, 1993).

We illustrate the application of story-based strategy to two concerns about transportation: going through airport security and flying on an airplane. You can easily use the steps to create stories tailored to your child and mode of transportation.

What to do before vacation

1. Identify the desired behavior – ***Going through airport security***

   Think about what specifically might be problematic for your child about this situation. Is it the noise, the large number of people, walking through the scanner, parting with his belongings as the bags are scanned?

   If your child tends to have strong reactions to noises, this might be an issue with the security check. If your child uses a wheelchair, he may be concerned how he will go through security with his wheelchair and whether he will have to get out of his wheelchair. If your child has a visual impairment, he might be concerned about how he will know when it is his turn to go through the metal detector or advanced imagining technology machine. If you child is deaf or hard of hearing, he may be concerned about being able to read the security officer's lips to understand what to do.

   Recall your discussion with your child from Step One. What led you to identify going through airport security as an issue? Have a discussion with your child about going through airport security, to see what aspects seem to be of greatest concern. These details will be important to address in the story you write.

   This activity can be adapted for other means of transportation. For example, if you need to ride a bus or subway to an attraction, your child will have to navigate the turnstile in the station and get on and off the subway.

2. Create a story "Going Through Airport Security."
   - Include an introduction, body, and conclusion.
   - Include who, what, when, where, how, and why. Include details appropriate to your child's age and the concerns you think your child might have about the situation.
   - Write in the first person. For example, "I will fly on an airplane when going on vacation."

- Use a combination of different types of sentence. Some of the types of sentences Carol Gray (1993) discusses using are descriptive and directive sentences.

  - Descriptive sentences describe what is happening in the situation and why. For example, when introducing the story about security, you might begin by writing, "Before boarding the airplane I will have to go through airport security. First I will wait in line. When I get to the security gate there will be an x-ray conveyor belt. The belt moves my suitcases through the x-ray machine."

    > ★ **Tip**
    >
    > According to the TSA children under 12 do not have to take off their shoes or light outerwear jackets.

  - Directive sentences tell the child what is expected of him in the situation. For example, when writing about preparing to go through the scanner, you might write, "I will take off my jacket and backpack and put them on the conveyer belt. Then I will walk through the scanner when the security officer tells me to."

★ **Tip**

When creating a story for a child who has an ambulatory disability, visual impairment, or who is or deaf or hard of hearing, refer to Chapter 2 – Determine Special Provisions Required for Travel, for information regarding TSA requirements for equipment and devices when going through airport security. Use this information to create a story with accurate information. For example, you can include statements such as, "The security officer will not ask me to remove my hearing aid when I go through security" to address some of your child's concerns.

- Write the story at your child's reading and comprehension level. For non-readers or a child with a visual impairment, consider creating an audio recording. Your child might follow along with the audio recording by looking at the book.
- Include photographs in the stories. If possible use actual photos of the interior and exterior of the airplane and airport. Many pictures can be downloaded from the airline Web site or by calling the marketing department to request photographs. For a child with a visual impairment, use large or raised pictures. Laminate pictures for durability, and keep in mind size, so the child can easily carry or keep it in a pocket. Lamination may not be appropriate for a child with a visual impairment due to glare. You can present the story to your child in several formats including:
  - On a single sheet of paper
  - On index cards
  - In a book
  - In an audio recording
  - In large print or Braille
  - On a smartphone or tablet

3. Review and discuss the story with your child on a regular basis beginning several weeks before the day you are traveling. Make sure you read the story with your child, especially the first few times. This will give you an opportunity to clarify and address any concerns he may have and also give your child a chance to ask questions. If your child can read on his own, encourage him to read the story. Leave the story in your child's room so he can have access to it whenever he wishes. As you read the story with your child, you may find that he has concerns about airport security you did not anticipate or write about. You may simply discuss those concerns or add them to your story.

4. Practice the skills discussed in the story at home before your trip. Pretend a doorway is a metal detector, or an advanced imagery technology machine. Set up a small

table for your personal items pretending it is the x-ray conveyor belt. Have someone (e.g., you, sibling) role-play being a security guard. If your child is able, have him place his bag on the table. Have your child wait on one side of the door/trellis until the "security officer" tells him to walk through. Have your child pick up his belongings on the small table after he goes through the scanner. Switch roles; some children will like the idea of role-playing the security guard and you the passenger. Explain to your child that sometimes the security officer may ask him to walk through the scanner a second time. Model for your child this procedure.

5. Reinforce appropriate behavior as your child complies with airport security procedures during practice sessions.

★ **Tips**

When you write the story, think about safety rules to keep your child safe in the airport. Safety rules are discussed later in this chapter. You may add your rules to the story to provide additional exposure.

The security gate can be busy with lots of people and backlogs of people waiting for their bags. You will have to move through the metal detector or advanced imagining technology machine separate from your child. To help ensure your child stays with you and also moves through the security machine successfully, consider making it a rule (and practicing this ahead of time) that you, another adult or older sibling with whom you are traveling goes first, then your child, and then another adult. This will ensure that familiar adults surround your child throughout the security process. Include this rule and way of navigating security in your story. Whatever rules you decide upon for things like going through airport security, make sure everyone knows and agrees on the rules. Discuss and practice those rules with your child.

What to do on vacation

- Be sure to bring your story with you on vacation.
- Review the story with your child on the way to the airport, while waiting in the check-in line, and when you are returning home.
- Just as you did when practicing, reinforce appropriately going through security at the airport. This means you should plan to bring reinforcers with you to the airport and have a plan for how, when, and for what behaviors you will provide them. You might provide a small item at each step in the security process (e.g., for waiting in line, putting bags on the scanner belt, walking through the scanner, retrieving bags on the other side) and/or a larger item at the end of the entire process. This could even be a treat at the airport while waiting to board the plane (e.g., a snack or magazine for the flight).

Stories can be applied to other travel concerns, as well as used to prepare your child for activities such as visiting an amusement park, zoo, or aquarium on vacation. Just remember that the story should include information about the attraction, what will happen at the attraction, emotions your child may experience, how to behave, and how to stay safe. As another example, we applied the story strategy to the concern about flying on an airplane.

> The story, "Going Through Airport Security," was written by Ms. J., for her daughter, Jane, who is a 7 year old child on the autism spectrum. Jane tends to wander, has difficulty waiting, and is reluctant to give up her personal items for fear of losing them. Ms. J. and Jane are planning to fly to Florida for vacation. Ms. J. includes information in the story about waiting for and boarding the airplane because these are also concerns for Jane.

Going Through Airport Security

I will fly on an airplane when I go on vacation. Before boarding the airplane I will have to go through airport security. I will take off my jacket and backpack and put them on the conveyer belt. I am worried the security officer will not give me back my stuff, but he will. The security officer will look at my bags through a special machine. After they have looked at my bags, I can take them back

I will stay close to my parents and wait for the security guard to tell me when it is my turn to walk through the scanner. I will listen to the security guard because he helps my parents keep me safe. The scanner will sound funny; it will beep when I walk through it. I have to remember to walk slowly through the scanner so the machine can do its job.

After I go through the scanner, I will pick up my bags. I will walk to the gate with my family. I will stay with my family at all times. I may have to wait to get on the plane. I do not like to wait, but I will try to be patient. I can look out the window at the airplanes, read a book, color, or play on my computer while I wait. When it is time to get on the plane, I will walk with my parents to the gate and hand my ticket to the airline representative. When I get to my seat, my parents will give me a surprise special treat.

Travel Concern - Flying on an Airplane
Intervention Strategy - Story

Flying on an airplane can be challenging. Your child will experience new sounds, close spaces, bright lights, and crowds. Your child will also be required to be patient and sit for a long period of time. It is difficult to anticipate what may happen and how your child will react on the flight, especially if your child has never flown before. As a parent, model appropriate behavior. Stay calm and show your child activities that he can do during the flight while waiting (e.g., read a book, listen to music, or work on a puzzle). For suggested activities review the section on waiting later in this chapter.

Another way to help prepare your child for flying is to intro-duce what happens when flying using a story. Just as with "Going

Through Airport Security" you can use the story to begin to discuss what happens when flying and then practice what will happen.

What to do before vacation
1. Identify desired behavior - *Flying on an airplane*
   Think about what specifically might be problematic for your child about this situation. Consider the following: being in enclosed in spaces, extremely small restrooms, narrow aisles, the sensation of pressure change, sitting still for long periods of time, loud engine noises, or sitting near unfamiliar people. If your child uses a wheelchair, he may be upset that he has to leave his wheelchair

> *Airplane specific wheelchair*
> – a narrow wheelchair that fits through the aisles on an airplane.

   when boarding the plane. He may not understand that he will get his wheelchair back once the plane lands. He may also be concerned about how he will move through the aisle to get to his seat or go to the bathroom.

Additional Information

If your child uses a wheelchair, add to the story statements about what will happen to your child's wheelchair. For example, "When I fly on an airplane I will leave my wheelchair at the gate. I am worried that I will not be able to get to my seat or the bathroom."
"I can use an *airplane specific wheelchair* to maneuver down the aisle to get to my seat and the bathroom.

---

2. Create a story "Flying on an Airplane."
   For directions to create a story refer to Step 2 of the previous activity, "Going Through Airport Security."

Your story should include general information about flying. The story should also include specific information to address your child's concerns. For example, if noise is a concern for your child, you might include statements such as, "The plane is going to be very noisy. The engine of the plane and the people around me will make noise. If the noise bothers me, I can put earplugs in my ears, or put on my headphones. I can also use relaxation techniques to calm myself."

3. Review and discuss the story beginning several weeks before the vacation.

4. Practice sitting on an airplane. As you read the story you may want to practice flying on an airplane.

   - If sitting for long periods of time is the primary issue with flying for your child, then practice sitting. Have your child practice sitting still. Start with a few minutes (begin with an amount of time that you know your child can accomplish with success). Pretend you are on an airplane. Praise success, and gradually increase the time. Have your child read or play hand held games. See section on waiting for activities.

   - If noises are an issue, add noises to the experience. Try to find a recording of airplane engines or loudspeakers. Go to a busy location that might simulate an airport waiting area or even to an actual airport and practice sitting quietly. Teach your child things to do to block the noise and remind him what to do if the noise is bothersome. You might consider providing him with earplugs or headphones and/or teaching him relaxation techniques. Relaxation techniques are described later in this chapter.

5. Reinforce appropriate behavior during practice sessions.

The story, "Flying on an Airplane," was written by Ms. R., for her son, Manuel, who is a 12 year old child on the autism spectrum. Manuel is sensitive to loud noises, becomes anxious when he has to do something for the first time, or when he is required to sit for long periods of time. Ms. R. and Manuel are planning to fly to California for vacation. Ms. R. includes information about what to expect when boarding an airplane, what he would be required to do during the flight, and activities to keep him busy while flying.

Flying on an Airplane

Sometimes when I go on vacation with my family I fly on an airplane. Going on an airplane is exciting, but also a little bit scary.

When it is time to board the airplane I will walk down a long hallway and then walk on the plane.

I will sit next to my parents. I will buckle my seatbelt and relax.

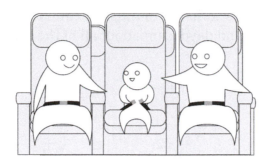

When the airplane is ready to take off it will go really fast and then soar into the air. It is a great feeling to be so high in the sky. Sometimes my ears will feel funny, but I will chew gum or suck on a lollipop to make them feel better.

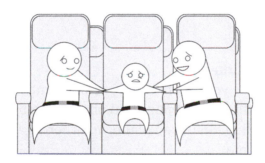

While on the airplane I may have a difficult time sitting still for so long. I can play video games, look out the window, read a book, have a snack, or take a nap.

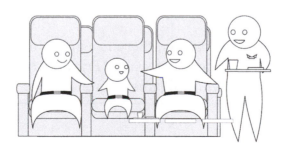

The plane may be very noisy. The engines of the plane and the people around me will make noise. If the noise bothers me, I will put on my headphones and listen to music. I can also practice my relaxation techniques and daydream about all of the fun I am going to have on vacation.

When the plane lands, I can get out of my seat and leave the airplane. I will listen to the flight attendant's instructions to stay safe. Disneyland here I come!

What to do on vacation

- Be sure to take your story with you on vacation.
- Review the story with your child on the way to the airport, before boarding, on the airplane, and then again before returning home.
- Use Behavior Specific Praise Statements to encourage appropriate behavior. For example: "Tommy, I really like the way you are sitting and playing on your computer."

★ **Tip**

If your child uses a computer, there is a great Internet interactive game about waiting in line, called *Eric Goes to the Airport*. It is available at www.whizkidgames.com.

Vacation Expectations

Part of the joy of traveling is all the new experiences, but this can also be part of the stress of traveling. With all the different experiences there are new expectations for your child's behavior. Your child may have limited experience with many situations he will encounter when traveling. In this section, we discuss several concerns related to expectations around new experiences and behavior for your child while on vacation.

Your child will have a smoother vacation if he practices ahead of time, this will help alleviate his worry about the new situations and prepare him with the necessary skills to navigate these new travel experiences.

Travel Concern - New Situations and Experiences – Riding on an Elevator
Intervention Strategy – Model and Practice

Children may show relatively mild behavior or extreme reactions to some new situations and experiences. Riding an elevator may be one new experience for your child when traveling. Some children may feel anxious and exhibit challenging behaviors when confined to closed spaces, or the feeling of going up and down on an elevator. A child who has only ridden an elevator once and was hesitant, may need more practice riding on an elevator before going on vacation. Use **model and practice** riding elevators to address this common travel concern.

Important Information
If your child shows significant fears or severe challenging behavior in some of these new situations, please consult a trained professional who has the experience and tools necessary to help you and your child with these situations.

What is model and practice?

Modeling is a strategy that involves showing or demonstrating a behavior. Practice involves presenting your child with opportunities to engage in a behavior where the situation is a more controlled environment than while on vacation. These opportunities will allow your child to gradually learn about, and get used to the new situations he may experience.

Why use model and practice to prepare for new situations on vacation?

Modeling and practicing for new situations can help your child learn appropriate behaviors. Use model and practice to break up the situation into smaller, more attainable goals. By using smaller steps, your child is more likely to be successful along the way.

How to use model and practice

1. Identify desired behavior.
2. Discuss and educate your child about the new situation.
3. Model and practice appropriate behavior for the new situation.
4. Reinforce and reassure your child's appropriate behavior with praise at every step.
5. Plan additional practice time.

What to do before vacation

1. Identify desired behavior - ***Riding on an elevator***
   Ultimately you want your child to ride an elevator from one floor to another. Your first goal may be for your child to stand near the elevator and watch it go up and down. Your next goal may be for your child to stand in the elevator without going up and down. Your final goal is then for your child to ride up and down the elevator at least one floor.
2. Discuss and educate your child about riding on an elevator. Set aside a quiet time and explain to your child that he will need to ride on an elevator when on vacation; there may be many cool things to see and do on vacation that might

require riding an elevator. Discuss how you will help him get used to this new experience by practicing before vacation. Educate your child about elevators. Present information in a way your child can understand, and at an age appropriate level. For example, if your child has never been on an elevator he may think that they go up and down really fast. In this situation read books and watch a video with your child about how elevators work. Have your child view Web site, "How Stuff Works" www.howstuffworks.com.

3. Model and practice appropriate behavior for riding on an elevator. Model riding on an elevator. Visit an office building or mall at an off peak time to allow your child a relatively calm environment to practice. You (or a sibling) can model going up and down the elevator. Have an adult stay with your child and explain what you are doing. Let your child imitate your modeled behavior. If this is a new experience, your child may readily board the elevator to practice. For children who are more hesitant, you might break this up into smaller steps. You might begin with asking your child to stand near the elevator while he does something enjoyable like eating a treat or playing with a favorite toy. When your child is successful standing near the elevator, have your child look inside the elevator. Then try getting on the elevator, but not riding it. Eventually, your child may ride the elevator one floor and then several floors at once.

4. Reinforce and reassure your child's appropriate behavior with praise at every step.
   You can use small items (e.g., a sticker or small bit of food) and/or Behavior Specific Praise Statements such as, "Enrique, good job riding one floor on the elevator today. I knew you could do it!"

5. Plan additional practice time.

What to do on vacation

- Continue to reassure your child when required to use the elevator.
- Remind him of his successful practice before vacation.
- Provide reinforcement for your child's appropriate behavior while riding the elevator.

If your child is still hesitant about riding an elevator (or any other new situation you identified for your vacation), consider making alternate arrangements such as staying at a smaller hotel or request a room on the first or second floor of a large hotel.

Travel Concern - New Situations and Experiences
Sleeping in a Different Bed
Intervention Strategy - Model and Practice

Travel disrupts routines including the time your child goes to bed, the actual bed in which your child sleeps, and the activities to prepare for bed. Most children are likely to feel unsettled if their bedtime routine is disrupted. This may be true for your child too.

Many children have a difficult time relaxing after a day of excitement, and may have difficulty falling asleep. This is magnified when sleeping in strange places. Maintaining bedtimes and nightly routines will help minimize the disruption. Adequate sleep will ensure that your child will not become over tired and cranky.

One disruption to bedtime on vacation is that your child will sleep in a different bed. You can begin to prepare your child for sleeping in a different bed by **modeling and practicing** this behavior and then having your child imitate you, to practice sleeping in a different bed.

What to do before vacation

1. Identify desired behavior - *Sleeping in a different bed*
   The goal of this activity is for your child to sleep in a different bed on vacation. You may need to set up mini-goals through-

out the practice period. Your first goal may be resting or reading in a different bed. When your child successfully rests in a different bed, the next goal may be sleeping in a different bed in your house. The next goal may be that your child sleeps at his grandparent's house.

2. Discuss and educate your child about sleeping in a different bed. Discuss that part of traveling is sleeping in a different bed. Help your child identify comfort items such as favorite books, stuffed animals, or a familiar blanket. Have the items near him when you discuss and begin modeling sleeping in a different bed. You can also talk about the room you will be staying in on vacation. If possible, show your child a picture of the room. By doing this your child will become familiar with the new sleeping arrangements. Discuss whether a sibling will be in the same room and/or where you will be if you will not be in the room. For a child with ambulatory disabilities or visual impairments, make sure to explain the physical layout of the room.

3. Model and practice sleeping in a different bed. Explain to your child that you (parent) will be sleeping in the guest room in your house to practice sleeping in a different bed while on vacation. If you do not have a guest room, you can switch beds with another child or sleep on the couch, just so you are modeling sleeping in a bed other than your own.

   ▪ Bring your pillow and blanket with you to the different bed.

   ▪ Follow your bedtime routine (e.g., laying in bed reading a book).

   ▪ Spend the night in the different bed. Your child should see you at least get ready to sleep and find you sleeping or just waking up in the new bed in the morning.

   In the morning, discuss how it felt sleeping in a different bed. For example, you may talk about how the bed felt -- maybe it was harder or softer. Talk about how the room looked different. Observe your child for worried or anxious behaviors such as biting lips, fidgeting, agitation, irritability, or withdrawal.

Have your child practice sleeping in a different bed. If your child shows some anxious behavior and/or seems uncomfortable with the idea of sleeping in a different bed, you should continue to model and break up the goal of sleeping in a different bed into smaller steps. One night you might just lie in the different bed with your pillow and blanket and have the child imitate just that behavior with his bedtime comfort items. The next night you might model lying in bed and reading; then have your child practice lying in the bed and reading a bedtime story (if this is part of your child's normal routine). The next night you might add turning out the light and falling asleep and have your child imitate to practice sleeping in the bed.

Even if sleeping in a different bed is not a concern for your child, make sure you identify and plan to bring his bedtime routine items and comfort items on vacation. These might include favorite books stuffed animals, blanket, and/or favorite pajamas.

4. Reinforce appropriate behavior at every step. Use praise and consider a special treat the next morning when your child sleeps through the night in a different bed.

5. Plan additional practice times for a few nights. Once your child successfully sleeps in a different bed in your home, you might have your child sleep in a bed away from home. This will be one step closer to the experience on vacation. This may be at a friend or relative's house, or a nearby hotel. Bring your child's comfort items that you plan to take on the trip, and listen to and observe your child's reactions, as this is key to understanding any issues that may arise once you are on vacation.

> ★ **Tip**
>
> If your child undergoes a time zone change make sure that you allow time to catch up on lost sleep and get acclimated to the new time schedule.

Jorge is a 12 year-old boy with Aspergers. Jorge's family is planning to visit his aunt in Houston, Texas. Jorge is routine oriented. He becomes upset when his daily routine is disrupted and when he does not have access to his personal belongings. Jorge's mother is concerned that the upcoming trip will be difficult for Jorge and the family. To help prepare Jorge for sleeping in a different bed his mother modeled and practiced this activity several weeks prior to the trip. First, she discussed the trip with Jorge and explained that he will be sleeping in his cousin's room at his aunt's house. She assured him that he could bring his bedtime comfort items with him on the trip (blanket, pillow, iPod). The next night Jorge's mother modeled sleeping in the guest room bed. She brought her blanket, pillow, and book. Jorge's mother explained to him what she was doing and stayed in the guest room bed until Jorge woke up in the morning, so he could see that she spent the night. Several days later Jorge's mother suggested that Jorge lie on the bed in the guest room after school and listen to his music on his iPod. Jorge stayed in the guest room until dinner. The next night Jorge's mother suggested that he should try sleeping in the guest room for one night. Jorge agreed, but only if he can take his personal items with him. Jorge fell asleep in the guest room until 2:00 a.m. and asked his mother if he could go back into his own bed. Jorge's mother suggested that he listen to his music and try to fall back to sleep. Jorge successfully slept in the guest room the remainder of the night.

What to do on vacation

- Remind your child that sleeping in a different bed is part of traveling.
- Remind your child that he slept in a different bed when you practiced at home.
- When you arrive at your hotel or cabin show your child around the room.
- When possible, give your child a choice of the bed in which he would like to sleep.
- Continue modeling by getting your new bed ready by putting your personal items on your bed.
- Let your child get his bed ready. He can place his comfort items on his bed and lay out his pajamas.
- Let him play on the bed with one of his favorite toys to become familiar with his new bed.
- Reinforce your child's preparing for bed and sleeping in his new bed.

Travel Concern - Transitioning From One Activity to Another
Intervention Strategy - Schedules

Traveling is full of transitions and new routines. There may also be unanticipated changes to plans. **Schedules** can be a very effective tool to aid with transitions.

What are schedules?

Schedules display the events and activities for a period of time. Schedules might display all the activities during a school day, or a set of steps or activities for a smaller period of time (e.g., the chores a child needs to complete before bedtime). We all use various kinds of schedules to plan our day (e.g. calendars, day planners, smartphones, grocery lists, to-do lists). Most of us would be lost without these schedules. A schedule is a visual support your child can check throughout the day to see what he has done and what he will do next. Schedules support a child's independence, transitioning, and active participation in the activities on the schedule. Schedules are effective with children of all ages. Schedules are also referred to as picture or activity schedules.

Why use schedules to help with transitioning from one activity to another?

With all the changes in routines and new activities when traveling, schedules can help convey what will happen and when. This may reduce challenging behavior associated with situations in which a child does not know what is happening next. Schedules can be made relatively portable, in small notebooks or photo books as well as on computers or phones. This is important when traveling.

How to use a schedule

1. Identify desired behavior.
2. Determine how you will record and display each activity on the schedule.
3. Create the schedule, putting events in sequential order. Include each activity you have planned.
4. Read the activity schedule with your child.
5. Require your child to carry his schedule on the day of the event and check it before and after each activity.
6. Reinforce checking the schedule as well as appropriate engagement in the activities on the schedule.

What to do before vacation

You can begin to prepare schedules prior to your vacation by following the first four steps of implementing a schedule. In the first four steps you will gather necessary materials to create schedules for use on vacation. You may be able to create some of the schedules (e.g., for the first day of your trip when you are traveling) before you leave for vacation, but it is unlikely that you will be able to create each day's schedule of activities in entirety before leaving for vacation.

★ **Tip**

If you child has never used a schedule, consider creating one that your child can follow during the days prior to going on vacation. For example, include going to school, going to the dentist, taking the bus, doing homework, having dinner, and preparing for bed.

---

1. Identify desired behavior - ***Transitioning from one activity to another***
2. Determine how you will record and display each activity on the schedule.
   Consider:

   - Mounting pictures on index cards (one picture on each card) or a piece of paper.
   - Typing or writing a schedule on an 8 ½" by 11" piece of paper.
   - Using stick figure drawings on a piece of paper.
   - Putting pictures in a small photo book.
   - Creating schedules by downloading iCommunicate and AA Visual Schedule apps on your iPad, iPod Touch, or iPhone.
   - Recording schedule on audio device.
     Print out pictures of the places you will be visiting on your vacation (e.g., zoo, hotel, museum, restaurant, playground). Visit the Web site of the places you will be visiting to obtain pictures to use on your child's schedule. Mount pictures on the schedule display. If your child is able to read, add short sentences about where you will be going, what will you be seeing, and how you will get there.
3. Create the schedule, putting the events in sequential order. Include each activity you planned. Example schedule:

On Tuesday we will
- ☐ Eat breakfast in the hotel restaurant with my family
- ☐ Drive to the aquarium
- ☐ Visit the aquarium and watch the fish

- ☐ Eat lunch in the café at the aquarium – special treat
- ☐ Go back to our hotel room and rest
- ☐ Walk to the playground
- ☐ Play at the playground
- ☐ Walk to the hotel
- ☐ Eat dinner at the pizzeria across the street
- ☐ Walk back to our hotel room and get ready for bed
- ☐ Follow bedtime routine
- ☐ Receive an extra bedtime story

4. Read the activity schedule with your child in the morning and before each activity.
   Check for understanding by having your child repeat back the information while pointing to the appropriate section of his schedule. When traveling, many times your schedule will change due to events out of your control; for example, a missed or canceled flight or a museum being closed. To prepare for a change in schedule, consider adding a change symbol or a special sticker, which means there will be change in plans. Teach your child about this ahead of time.
5. Require your child to carry his schedule with him and check his schedule as each activity ends. Use verbal and visual cues to remind him to check his schedule. Should your schedule change, update the schedule with your child.
6. Reinforce checking the schedule.

Dion is a 9 year old boy with a physical disability. He spends the majority of his day in a wheelchair. When Dion's mother discussed their vacation in Step One, she noted Dion was quite concerned about the various places they would be going and asked lots of questions about his wheelchair. He was concerned if he would have to leave his wheelchair at home, how it would fit on the airplane, and what type of van they would drive while on vacation. To help Dion with the various transitions, his mother created a schedule. Before creating Dion's schedule, his mother visited the Web sites of the various attractions and accommodations to confirm that all destinations were accessible. She then created a schedule that clearly reflected these special provisions. As Dion viewed his schedule he noticed that his family was traveling in a wheelchair accessible van, ramps were located throughout the zoo, the restrooms at the zoo and restaurants were wheelchair accessible and he would be visiting a Boundless PlaygroundTM discussed in Chapter 1. Dion's mother created a schedule using pictures in a small spiral notebook that will be easily attached to his wheelchair.

What to do on vacation
- Take materials (from steps 2 and 3) with you to make schedules. You may also plan to use what you have available in your hotel room to create a simple handwritten schedule.
- While on vacation, follow steps 3-6 about creating and using the schedules.
- Create final schedules for those days' activities and plans that you had not finalized before leaving for vacation (e.g., exactly what you will do on Tuesday may be decided on Monday night depending upon whether everyone finished visiting the zoo on Monday, or wants to return to see more of the zoo on Tuesday).

Strategies to Support Successful Transitions

Provide a **warning**. Have your child check the schedule before transition time and provide a verbal or visual warning about the impending transition. For example, 5 minutes before leaving the playground for dinner have your child check the schedule and say, "In 5 minutes we are leaving for dinner." If your child has difficulty with the concept of time, give your child a watch with a timer to count down. You can also count down the minutes on your fingers. For some children a 2 minute warning works fine, for others they transition better with a longer warning period (e.g., 10 minutes).

Provide a **preferred item as a distracter**. As your child checks the schedule, you can offer a preferred toy or activity that may provide distraction from the difficult transition. For example, as your child checks the schedule you might offer to let him listen to his iPod on the walk back to the hotel.

Provide a **choice** about the transition. As your child checks the schedule offer a choice about the impending transition. For example, you might offer different ways to leave the park and get to the hotel for dinner, saying, "Do you want to walk by the fountain or look in the store windows?"

To use these strategies successfully, remember to provide warnings, distractions, and choices when your child begins the transition and before he engages in challenging behavior.

Travel Concern - Overstimulation at Attractions
Intervention Strategy - Relaxation Techniques

Traveling and attractions are filled with noises, smells, bright lights, and sights that can easily overwhelm your child if they are hypersensitive. Walking on crowded city streets, your child will be exposed to people talking, yelling, sirens blaring, people bumping into each other, and different food smells from street vendors. Amusement parks are filled with fun rides, loud music, and flashing lights.

To minimize your child becoming overwhelmed, travel during off peak hours and season if possible. This may reduce the number of people and some of the stimulation. Your child can also wear earplugs and sunglasses to curtail noise and visual stimulation. Plan to take frequent breaks in a quiet area.

In spite of all your efforts, your child may still become overwhelmed. Children typically do not have the skills that most adults have learned in order to manage stressors. Consider preparing your child with **relaxation techniques**.

What are relaxation techniques?

Relaxation techniques involve focusing attention on something to reduce stress and anxiety. There are several different types of relaxation techniques. Relaxation techniques may improve self-regulation, sensory overload, and emotional regulation. These techniques are easy to learn and can be practiced with your child often. The more experience your child has with the technique, the easier it becomes to use when necessary in a stressful situation.

Why use relaxation techniques to help with overstimulation at attractions?

We chose relaxation techniques to address this situation because practicing relaxation can help your child remain calm, and reduce the likelihood of escalating to a challenging behavior like panic or aggression.

Relaxation techniques need to be taught in advance so your child can use the technique before becoming upset on vacation. Detection of your child's physical signs of stress and triggers requires observation and communication with your child. Once you are aware of your child's triggers, then you will be able to intervene and encourage him to use one of his relaxation techniques before his behavior escalates.

How to use relaxation techniques
1. Identify desired behavior.
2. Choose a relaxation technique to teach your child.
3. Follow the steps to teach one of the relaxation techniques.
4. Practice relaxation regularly.

What to do before vacation
1. Identify desired behavior - ***Engage in the relaxation technique***
2. Choose a relaxation technique to teach your child.
   We describe three relaxation techniques: belly breathing, progressive muscle relaxation, and visualization. Review the techniques below and choose at least one to teach to your child. The relaxation technique you choose will depend on several factors: your child's disability, preference, ease of practice, whether it fits into planned activities, and which produces the best results for your child.
3. Follow the steps to teach one of the relaxation techniques.
4. Practice relaxation regularly and when your child is calm and not upset or anxious.

Belly Breathing

The main focus of belly breathing is to slow down breathing and deepen each breath. Belly breathing is also referred to as diaphragmatic breathing. Lori Lite's Web site, www.stressfreekids.com, contains additional information about belly breathing.

- Begin by asking your child to lie on his back and place one hand on his belly. After your child learns to use belly breathing, he can practice it sitting and standing so that it will be easier for him to use it in many different situations on vacation.
- Ask your child to take a slow deep breath in through his nose and let it out through his mouth with a gentle "ah-h-h-h-h" sound. He should breath in for a count of 4 and out for a count of 4; you might say, "In, 2, 3, 4 and out, 2, 3, 4" to

help him breath slowly. He should feel his belly rise and fall with his hand.

- Have your child do this several times.
- Practice on a daily basis at a time when your child is not anxious or upset.
- Reinforce successfully following your instructions for practicing relaxation.

Progressive Muscle Relaxation

With progressive muscle relaxation, your child will focus on slowly tensing and then relaxing each muscle group. One method of progressive muscle relaxation is to start by tensing and relaxing the muscles in your toes. Then slowly move up your body, tensing and relaxing all the muscles, all the way up to your neck and head. You can also start with your head and work down to your toes (Mayo Clinic, 2011).

Before practicing progressive muscle relaxation, consult with your child's doctor to ensure your child does not have any medical issues that may be aggravated by tensing his muscles.

- Ask your child to sit in a comfortable position with both feet on the floor.
- Ask your child to take several deep breaths in and then slowly blow out.
- Tell your child you will ask him to squeeze different parts of his body for 10 seconds and then release the squeeze.
  - Start with the toes and work up the body or you can start from the top and work your way down.
  - Have your child concentrate on his right foot, have him squeeze his foot and toes for 10 seconds, and then relax.
  - Move to his left foot, have him squeeze his foot and toes for 10 seconds, then relax.
  - Move up to the right calf, squeeze for 10 seconds, and then relax.
  - Move to the knee, upper leg and thigh each for 10 seconds, and then relax.

- Move to the left calf, squeeze for 10 seconds, and then relax.
- Move to the knee, upper leg and thigh each for 10 seconds, and then relax.
- Move up to the buttock. Squeeze tightly for 10 seconds, and then relax.
- Next move up to the stomach; squeeze the stomach muscles tight for 10 seconds, then release.
- Tense the right hand, make a fist, and hold for 10 seconds, then release. Squeeze the right lower arm, elbow and bicep. Hold for 10 seconds, and then relax.
- Tense the left hand, make a fist, and hold for 10 seconds, then release. Squeeze the left lower arm, elbow and biceps. Hold for 10 seconds, and then relax.
- Tense shoulders by pointing them upward to the ears, hold for 10 seconds, then relax.
- Tense the chest for 10 seconds, and then relax.
- Tense back muscles, hold for 10 seconds, and then relax.
- Next, move to the neck, squeeze tightly for 10 seconds, and then relax.
- Tense the entire face for 10 seconds, and then relax.
- Squeeze eyes shut for 10 seconds, and then relax.
- Finally, tense the entire body. Hold for 10 seconds, then release.
- For children who have difficulty with oral directions create a sequence of pictures to describe the process. Using an audio device with headphones may also be a way for your child to be able to use this relaxation technique independently.
- For younger children, you can have them tense their muscles for several seconds.
- Practice on a daily basis at a time when your child is calm.
- Reinforce successfully following your instructions for practicing relaxation.

Visualization

Did you know your child could calm himself by visualizing his favorite smells, places, or activities? Visualization is another technique to reduce stress. It is easy to use and your child can use it anywhere. All your child needs is his own imagination. One of our favorites for younger children is this simple and effective exercise:

- Ask your child to sit in a comfortable chair and close his eyes.
- Ask your child to take a few slow deep breaths.
- Ask him, "What is your favorite smell, place, or activity?" If he can't think of anything give a few ideas: pizza, chocolate, popcorn, candy, French fries, cotton candy, flowers, the park, beach, skiing, his bedroom.
- Ask your child to breathe in through his nose for 4 seconds, hold for 2 seconds, and exhale through his mouth for 6 seconds. For younger children, have them breathe in using a 2-in, 1-hold, and 3-out set. You can even count with or for your child. Count quietly to help your child slowly breathe in and out. Every time he inhales, tell him to think of his favorite smell, place, or activity.
- Practice on a daily basis at a time when your child is calm.
- Reinforce successfully following your instructions for practicing relaxation.

★ **Tip**

Read with your child "Bubble Riding" by Lori Lite. This book enhances visualization through relaxation stories. Visit www.stressfreekids.com for more information.

What to do on vacation
- Relaxation techniques can be used anywhere and anytime when you are on vacation. When teaching your child a relaxation technique, we suggest finding a quiet place.

This is not always possible on vacation. If your child shows signs of becoming anxious, find a quiet bench, the back of a restaurant /food court, or otherwise out of the way spot to allow your child a quiet space to practice relaxation. Remind your child to use the technique(s) he has learned.

Jada is an 8 year old girl who is hard of hearing. She becomes over stimulated and starts to cry at busy attractions due to loud noises. Jada's mother wants to take the family to an amusement park, but is concerned that Jada will have difficulty coping with the loud noise. Jada's mom recalls that her daughter's teacher is teaching Jada Progressive Muscle Relaxation to use when the bell rings. Jada's mother practices this technique at home to reinforce what Jada is doing at school. Once Jada was comfortable using this technique, her mother added background music and reminded her to begin her relaxation technique. When on vacation, Jada's mother watches for signs of overstimulation. Jada's mother takes her to a quiet area and prompts her to use Progressive Muscle Relaxation.

Travel Concern - Waiting
Intervention Strategy - W.A.I.T. Box

Waiting is a necessary life skill and a big part of traveling. Your child may need to wait on line at an attraction, to board a plane or cruise ship, to catch a taxi, or to be served in a restaurant. Waiting requires self -control, concentration, and understanding time. Children may not possess all of these skills at an early age. Just like every skill, waiting needs to be learned and practiced. One way to support your child while he waits when traveling is to prepare your child with activities and fun things to do while he waits. Even adults have to occupy themselves when they wait. They read a book or magazine, check their messages or e-mails on their phone, or have a conversation with another person. Create and use a **W.A.I.T. Box** on vacation to occupy your child's time while waiting.

What is a W.A.I.T. Box?

A W.A.I.T. Box is an activity box or bag to help your child occupy his time when he is required to wait. The activities and toys included will depend on the child's age and interests. W.A.I.T. stands for:

- **W**atch something
- **A**rts and crafts
- **I**nclude your child's favorite things
- **T**ake your child's favorite games

Why use a W.A.I.T. Box to help with waiting?

A W.A.I.T. Box is put together with your child's interests and abilities in mind. It is portable and will provide your child with activities to do while he waits. The activities provide a distraction from the otherwise boring activity of waiting.

How to use a W.A.I.T. Box

1. Identify desired behavior.
2. Discuss with your child what waiting means.
3. Brainstorm with your child what he could do if he had to wait.
4. Create a W.A.I.T. Box.
5. Practice using the W.A.I.T. Box at home.
6. Reinforce your child's use of the W.A.I.T. Box and appropriate waiting.

What to do before vacation

1. Identify desired behavior - *Waiting*
2. Discuss with your child what waiting means. The meaning can be as simple as saying, "Waiting means you can sit or stand quietly even when you are very excited." Explain to your child that waiting is part of life and that you will need to wait when traveling and while on vacation.

3. Brainstorm with your child what he could do if he had to wait. Explain to your child what you do when you have to wait (e.g. listen to music, read, check e-mails on your phone).
   Provide specifics related to travel such as waiting at an amusement park, a restaurant, and at the airport.

4. Create a W.A.I.T. Box. Identify a container in which to put the items your child can use while waiting. This container could be a small box, bag, backpack, or fanny pack. Make the container something special. Identify items to include in the W.A.I.T. Box. Include items that your child plays with regularly. You may want to add a few new items to the box as a surprise. Sometimes novelty is the best distraction. Make sure the items are portable enough to fit in the container and appropriate for your child to use while waiting (e.g. not too noisy). Also take into consideration any of your child's special needs (e.g., choose visually interesting items for a child with who is deaf or hard of hearing). Make sure to include a variety of different items to maintain your child's interest.
   Suggestions:
   - **W**atch something. Your child might watch his favorite movies or shows on a portable DVD player, computer, or tablet.
   - **A**rts and crafts are fun and easy activities to occupy a child when waiting. Pack coloring books, sketchpads, markers, and crayons.
   - **I**nclude your child's favorite things: book, stuffed animal, doll.
   - **T**ake your child's favorite games: Tic -Tac-Toe, cards, hangman, Braille playing cards, and word games.

5. At home, prior to your trip, practice using the W.A.I.T. Box on short outings to the grocery store, the pharmacy, or a restaurant. When your child needs to wait, prompt him to take out and use an item from his W.A.I.T. Box.

6. Reinforce your child's use of the W.A.I.T. Box and appropriate waiting.

What to do on vacation
- Bring your child's W.A.I.T. Box with you on vacation.
- Prompt your child to use his W.A.I.T. Box when required to wait on vacation. Remember, prompt your child to use his W.A.I.T. Box as soon as he is required to wait (e.g. as soon as you sit down at the restaurant) to prevent challenging behaviors while waiting.

Travel Concern - Eating at a Restaurant and Etiquette Intervention Strategy - Video Modeling and Practice

Eating in restaurants is inevitable when traveling. Children may have difficulty with this change in routine, the new environment in a restaurant, and/or eating different foods. Children might not be accustomed to eating in restaurants. At home, mealtimes are served quickly, but not in many restaurants.

Expectations for behavior are different than at home. At home, it may be acceptable for your child to get up from his seat during mealtime, watch television, and/or talk loudly. In a restaurant, acceptable behavior is defined differently and different rules apply.

What is video modeling?

Video modeling is a mode of teaching that uses video recording and display equipment to provide a visual model of the targeted behavior or skill (Franzone & Collet-Klingenberg, 2008). Your child will observe someone else or himself perform each step of an appropriate behavior and then have the opportunity to imitate the behavior.

Why use video modeling to help with restaurant etiquette?

We chose video modeling because it is an effective approach to teaching a new behavior. Your child can view, imitate, and practice the new behavior at home before trying it in a restaurant. It also gives you the option to pause and analyze specific skills with your child. Many children enjoy watching television; so video modeling can be a fun activity. We have found children enjoy being recorded and seeing themselves on video. However, if your child does not like to watch television or video-recorded materials, this strategy may not be as effective. Video modeling is appropriate to use with children of a wide range of ages and abilities. To use video modeling while traveling, put your videos on a laptop, tablet, or smartphone to view conveniently just before going to a restaurant.

How to use video modeling

1. Identify the desired behavior.
2. Write a script that targets the skill or behavior you want to teach.
3. Select models. This can be your child (referred to as video self-modeling), a family member, or peer.
4. Select a setting (e.g. restaurant, living room, kitchen, dining room) for your video.
5. Use a recording device to record the model.
6. Edit the video.
7. View the video with your child and have your child imitate the appropriate behavior at home.
8. View the video and practice in a real life setting. Reinforce appropriate behaviors.

What to do before vacation

1. Identify desired behavior - ***Restaurant etiquette***
   Appropriate restaurant behaviors include sitting in the chair with feet on the floor, talking in a quiet-inside voice, using utensils to eat food, putting one bite in mouth at a time, using a napkin to wipe mouth, and saying thank you when the food is served.

2. Write a script that targets the skill or behavior you want to teach. The script should reflect the aspects of restaurant etiquette identified for your child. Write the script exactly the way you want it said and demonstrated in the video. Include verbal and nonverbal cues, such as body language and facial expression. To hold your child's attention, keep the video short (e.g., under 2 minutes).

3. Select models. This can be your child (video self-modeling), a family member or peer.
   Make sure your model can precisely follow your script. If your child is the model, any inappropriate behaviors need to be removed during the editing process. If you are not comfortable videotaping and editing, there is an informative article that may help you by Dr. Tom Buggey, *A Picture Is Worth...Video Self-Modeling Applications at School and Home.* Buggey explains self-video modeling and how to create videos using VCR or computer software.

4. Select a setting for your video. It would be best if you could record the model illustrating restaurant etiquette in a restaurant. If this is not possible, create a restaurant like atmosphere in your home. Set the table with placemats or a tablecloth. Put menus on the table. Have someone play the role of a server and ask for your food order, bring your food, and clear away the dishes.

5. Use a recording device to record the model. Record only after the model is prepared and comfortable. Record several sessions. Additional information about how to make videos for video modeling can be found on the Web site "Video Modeling: A Visual Teaching Method for Children

with Autism" by Lisa Neumann (www.ideasaboutautism.com/video.html).

6. Edit the video. Cut out any inappropriately modeled table manners. Remember you want the desired behavior modeled correctly. Keep the edited video under 2 minutes. Developments in technology have simplified the editing process. There are many free and easy to use video-editing programs available for download. If you use Apple devices, *iMovie* can be purchased from the App Store and allows you to edit and then download your video to an iPod, iPad, or iPod touch. Microsoft also offers *Windows Live Movie Maker* as a free download that allows you to edit videos on your PC. Easy step-by-step tutorials are available on-line.

7. View the video with your child and have him imitate the appropriate behavior at home. Reinforce appropriate behaviors. Show the video several times and discuss and point out appropriate restaurant behavior. Pause the video to discuss any part in more detail. After your child watches the video, set up a practice opportunity at home. Pretend you are having dinner at a restaurant. Set the table with a formal appearance if you will be dining at a formal restaurant, or obtain a sample menu (one from a local restaurant or the Internet can be used as an example). Have someone play the hostess and server. Practice ordering food, waiting, eating the food when it arrives, and waiting for the check. Reinforce appropriate behaviors.

8. View the video and practice in a real life setting. After your child is successful eating during practice at home, practice at a local restaurant. Put your video on a portable device (e.g., laptop, DVD player, smartphone) to show your child just prior to entering the restaurant.
    -   View the video.
    -   Visit a restaurant with relatively quick service, and plan to have a short meal. Order an appetizer or desert to see how your child handles dining out for a short period of time. If your child has difficulty sitting in a restaurant

for an entire meal, it may be a good idea to order your dinner to go and an appetizer to eat at the restaurant while you wait. If you do this at the hotel restaurant, you can avoid high room service prices.

- Reinforce appropriate behavior in the restaurant.

What to do on vacation

- Video models are intended to be viewed immediately before the situation, in this case, eating in a restaurant. On vacation this might be difficult if your video models are on a computer or DVD, but can be much easier if you download the videos to your smartphone, tablet, or a similar portable device that you can carry with you while traveling. With today's technology, bringing a device to review the video clip is easy and convenient. If you do not have the portable technology, take still photos from the video demonstrating appropriate restaurant etiquette.
- Review the video with your child prior to going to the restaurant.
- Reinforce your child's appropriate behavior. For example, before leaving for the restaurant discuss with your child that he will receive a special treat after dinner if he follows the restaurant rules practiced at home. Make sure your child knows exactly what is expected of him. For example "If you follow restaurant rules, you will earn a special dessert."

★ **Tips**

Choose child friendly restaurants with:

> Relaxed, noise tolerant atmospheres
> Children's menus
> Highchairs and booster seats
> Coloring books and crayons
> Outside tables

At some restaurants you can make reservations as well as order your meals ahead of time to lessen the wait.

Visit the Web site of the restaurant to make sure they have a meal your child will eat.

Check that special provisions are available for allergies/dietary needs.

Bring quiet interactive activities that your child can do while waiting for his meal (e.g., books, small puzzles, hand held video games). Use your child's W.A.I.T. Box if you have one; see section on waiting in this chapter.

Break up wait time by taking short walks in the front area of the restaurant. Take these walks before your child engages in challenging behavior because he has been waiting at the table too long.

Have your child practice relaxation techniques.

You can help prepare your child for eating in restaurants by reading books about the topic. Some children's books related to eating in restaurants are:

Barney and Baby Bop Go to the Restaurant by Lyrick Publishing

Caillou at a Fancy Restaurant by Sarah Margaret Johnson.

Travel Concern - Following Morning/Evening Routine Intervention Strategy – Mini Schedule

Accommodating your child's everyday routines during a vacation can be as simple as maintaining mealtimes, bedtimes, and certain play activities your child has come to expect as part of his daily routine. You can help maintain a sense of order and stability by teaching your child to use a **mini schedule** for managing some of his activities during the day.

What is a mini schedule?

A mini schedule is a way of breaking up a task or activity into smaller steps that your child follows in order to complete that task. Mini schedules can be added to a schedule you may have for your child's day (see the section about schedules earlier in this chapter). Mini schedules can provide more detailed information about an activity that is on the child's daily schedule. For example, your child's daily schedule may include "morning routine." A companion mini schedule for morning routine lists the specific tasks you child needs to do in the morning (e.g., use bathroom, brush teeth, take off pajamas).

Why use a mini schedule to address following morning/evening routine?

Mini schedules help children complete an activity by breaking the activity down into steps. The schedule also provides a way to illustrate changes in routine that are likely to happen on vacation. Mini schedules are portable and easy to use on vacation. As children learn to follow schedules, they become more independent. Mini schedules can help maintain a sense of order and familiarity while away from home.

How to use a mini schedule

1. Identify desired behavior.
2. Create a mini schedule.

3. Place the mini schedule in the area where you child will have to complete a task.
4. Teach your child to use a mini schedule.
5. Reinforce following the mini schedule and completing the task(s).

What to do before vacation
1. Identify desired behavior - ***Following morning/evening routine***.
   Break down the task into simple, concise, manageable steps, for example:

Morning Mini Schedule
Use bathroom
Take pajamas off
Put on underpants
Put on pants
Button pants
Put on shirt
Button shirt
Put on socks
Put on shoes
Brush teeth
Take medication
Eat breakfast

Evening Mini Schedule
Take off clothes
Bath/shower
Put on pajamas
Take medication
Brush teeth
Read a story
Practice relaxation techniques

2. Create a mini schedule.

   You may want to include your child in creating the schedule. If you are using pictures or photos make sure they are clear and focus on the task to be completed. For example, if you want your child to brush his teeth, include a picture or photo of the toothpaste, toothbrush, cup, and sink rather than the entire bathroom.

   Schedules can be created by:

   - Writing or typing the steps on a piece of paper
   - Using clip art
   - Using photos of your child completing the task
   - Pairing pictures/photos with written text
   - Writing on a dry erase board (this type of schedule can be quickly put together and easily modified if there are changes)
   - Using PECS mini schedule board with pictures (www. pecsproducts.com), if your child is familiar with these symbols
   - Using an audio recording on a smartphone or tablet

3. Place the mini schedule in the area where your child will need to complete the tasks.

   For example, most morning routines take place in the bathroom, so it may be a good idea to tape the mini schedule on the inside of the bathroom door or on the wall next to the sink in your room.

4. Teach your child to use a mini schedule. Before and during vacation practice using the mini schedule with your child. Prompt your child to look at the schedule, point to the next step, complete next step, and return to schedule. To encourage independence, teach your child how to self-manage using a mini schedule. See self-management tip box.

5. Reinforce following the mini schedule and completing the task/activity.

Using a mini schedule to self-manage morning/evening routines
A mini schedule is a perfect tool to use as part of self-management. Your child may become proficient with his mini schedule and need less and less of your assistance. You can encourage your child's independent use of the schedule by adding a way for your child to mark the completion of each step. For example, adding a box or line for child to check off the completion of the step fosters self-management.

What to do on vacation

- Bring copies of the morning/evening mini schedules with you on vacation. Make sure you have materials to modify the schedule if needed.
- Post the mini schedule in a visible location where your child can see and reach it if needed.
- Provide a reinforcer for using the schedule and completing the schedule task/activity.

★ **Tip**

If your child has a visual impairment, provide your child with a mini schedule in large print or Braille.

Interacting with Others

There are many social interaction skills that are necessary when traveling. Your child may meet and talk with new people such as flight attendants and hotel personnel. He may meet new relatives or visit relatives he sees infrequently. At children's programs, your child may need to play with other children. The new people and types of interactions can be difficult for many children, including those with special needs. In this section we discuss strategies to address some common concerns about social interaction when traveling.

Travel Concern: Conversing with Different People
Intervention Strategy - Visual Script

When traveling, there will be times when your child will be expected to make requests, answer questions, and greet/respond appropriately to different people. Interacting with new people presents with a variety of challenges. Some of these individuals may not understand or have experience with your child's disability. Sometimes it is difficult for new people to understand the way a child communicates. Children may be anxious or have difficulty engaging in conversations and social interactions. You can help prepare your child for social interactions using **Visual Scripts.**

★ **Tip**

Your child will come in contact with many different people while you are traveling. Whether it is a family member, an airport security officer, or a hotel employee, their awareness and understanding of your child's disability can contribute to successful interaction. There are several ways to inform family or staff about your child's disability. If possible, the best way to share information about your child would be through conversation with the people involved. Keep information simple and informative. Describe your child's special needs, his strengths, and the best way to communicate with him. You can also print business cards that provide information about your child's disability and special needs to distribute. These can be especially useful when you are unable to speak to the person directly. As a useful example, ready-made Autism Awareness Cards are available through the Autism Society.

What is a visual script?

Visual scripts are phrases or sentences that will provide your child with socially appropriate phrases he can use to

> ***Prompt*** – a cue given to help remember what to say or do

communicate with others. The visual script provides a *prompt* for appropriate communicative behavior that the child reads.

Why use a visual script to help converse with different people on vacation?

Visual scripts can be used with children with communication impairments, social deficits, learning disabilities and/or cognitive impairments. Visual scripts can be used with children who are able to read. For non-readers you can use puppets to model a social interaction or create picture scripts. Audiotaped scripts can be used for those with visual impairments. Visual scripts are easy to use, can be modified to suit your child's age and abilities, and support language development.

How to use a visuals script

1. Identify desired behavior.
2. Write the script.
3. Create a way to display the script for your child to read.

> ***Fade*** – decrease the level of assistance to complete a task or activity

4. Practice the script with your child.
5. Reinforce your child's participation.
6. *Fade* the script over time and/or prepare to bring the script with you to the activity.

What to do before vacation

A few months prior to vacation you may want to begin thinking about with whom your child will come in contact on vacation. This is a good time to start creating visual scripts for these types of situations. For example, your child may need to talk with peers in a children's program, speak with the server when ordering food at a restaurant, and ask the hotel personnel where is the location of the game room.

1. Identify desired behavior - ***Converse with different people***
   Where it will take place? On a cruise ship, at a hotel, in a restaurant, on the beach, or at an attraction. With whom? Greeting a peer on the playground or beach, asking for help, ordering food, and asking for a beach toy.
2. Write the visual script.
   Depending on where, when, and with whom your child will converse, you may need to create several visual scripts. Your child may need a script to order food at a restaurant, to converse with children in a playroom, at a pool, or to ask for a drink on an airplane.

   What does your child need to say in each of the situations? You might observe typically developing peers so you are aware of words/phrases to use when writing your child's scripts.

   You can write the script with your child and prepare it ahead of time. If you write the script with your child, begin by telling him that you are going to write or use pictures to create a script he can use when he is unsure of what to say to someone. Explain that together you will write the script. For example, if you want to write a script about asking another child at the park to play, you might tell your child, "You are going to pretend mommy is a child that you meet at the park. We will describe with words what you are going to say when you want to play with the child."
   Writing the script:
   - Create a scenario of two children having a conversation. Choose a place and activity.
   - Write a scenario in dialogue form. The length of the phrases will depend on your child and his reading and speaking ability.

- Be sure to include kind and polite greetings and words when talking to other people you may meet, e.g., "thank you," "it was nice meeting you," "you're welcome," "how are you?"

3. Create a way to display the script for your child to read. Scripts can be displayed on a piece of paper like a play, in a book, a small photo album, on a key ring for easy transport, or even on a phone, laptop or tablet. Scripts can also be recorded on a portable recording device or a phone for your child to listen to just before interacting with someone.

    To create a script on a key ring, print the script in large enough print that your child can read easily. Cut the printed phrases into strips. Laminate the strips and punch a hole in the end of each strip. Attach the strips to a key ring. Your child can wear the key ring and use it as a reminder of what to say. Here is an example of a script for interacting with a new child at the park:

Child:	Hi.
Parent:	Hi.
Child:	What's your name?
Parent:	My name is_____. What's your name?
Child:	_____.What are you playing?
Parent:	I am playing_____.
Child:	Can I play too?
Parent:	Scenario 1 –Yes.
Child:	Cool.
Parent:	Scenario 2 – No, you can't play.
Child:	Okay (stay calm, move, and start a conversation with another child).

4. Practice the script with your child. Role-play with your child to allow him to practice reading the script. Pretend you are in the relevant situation (e.g., pretend you are a peer at the playground by practicing in your backyard on the swings). You may have to prompt your child to read the script. Prompting may include pointing to the script or providing a model of what the child is supposed

to read and say. When your child is able to read through the script without prompts, you may want him to practice with siblings, friends, or other family members.

5. Reinforce your child's participation.
6. Fade the script over time and/or prepare to bring the script with you on vacation to help him interact with others. The visual script acts as a prompt for your child to interact in social situations. As your child learns to read the script without your prompts, you may also be able to fade the use of the script. Fade the script by removing a portion of the script (e.g., the last word or phrase). To begin fading the sample script from step 3, you might start by removing the final phrase, "Cool." Keep practicing and if your child continues to say thank you, then you can remove the next to last phrase, "Can I play too?" Continue this until the entire script is removed. Monitor your child's progress. Be prepared to back-up if your child does not continue to say the entire script. If you do not have time to fade the script, bring it with you on vacation.

What to do on vacation

- Review the visual scripts regularly while on vacation. You can review and practice before the scripted situation. For example, on the day you visit family members with several small children, practice the script for playing with peers; on the day you ride the train, practice the script for interacting with the conductor to hand over your ticket.
- If your child forgets to use his script, you may have to prompt him to do so. For example, when the flight attendant approached Sally to offer her a snack, Sally's mother pointed to the key chain on Sally's waistband. When the flight attendant asked Sally, "Can I get you something to drink?" Sally readily responded apple juice and thanked the flight attendant.
- Reinforce your child's appropriate communication and use of the script.

Sally, a 10 year old girl with multiple disabilities, is going on vacation with her family. Sally uses speech to communicate, but her speech is often difficult for others to understand. With practice, Sally can effectively communicate short phrases so that others understand her. Sally's mother creates scripts for Sally to practice communicating with some of the people with whom she would need to interact with on their trip. For example, Sally's mother creates a script of a conversation with the flight attendant on the airplane so Sally could order something to drink:

Flight attendant: May I get you something to drink?
Sally: Apple juice, please.
Flight attendant: Apple juice?
Sally: Yes, please.
Flight attendant: Here you go.
Sally: Thank you.

Sally's mother writes other scripts for different interactions, including greeting kids at the pool, restaurant servers, and hotel staff. Because one of the concerns for Sally was not being understood, Sally's mother also includes practice for what to do when the person with whom Sally was speaking did not understand her (e.g., Sally told a peer she wanted to play ball, but the peer did not understand; Sally practiced repeating her words and even showing what she was saying by pointing to the ball).

Travel Concern - Meeting Unfamiliar Relatives
Intervention Strategy - Scrapbook

When meeting someone new, some children will be excited and others will become anxious and resistant. Your child may see a visit to a family member as a social demand, thus creating anxiety. Part of helping your child in this situation will be to prepare your relatives in advance. Prior to your visit, contact them to discuss your child's special needs. If your child has difficulty interacting with unfamiliar people, your relatives may not understand your child's behaviors and feel slighted. Be specific and explain how your child's disability affects his behavior, communication, social interactions, and food preferences. To further ensure your family will understand your child's needs, you may consider sending them literature about your child's disability. If you explain in advance, they are more likely to understand your child's disability.

Even with preparation, meeting unfamiliar relatives may be difficult for your child. He may not know what to say when unfamiliar relatives ask questions about his favorite activities, school, grade level, or best friend. To help prepare your child for sharing information about himself with unfamiliar relatives, create a **scrapbook** to bring on vacation.

★ Tip

You can also use the scripting strategy discussed previously, to help your child learn what to say to converse with relatives.

What is a scrapbook?
A scrapbook is a photo album that contains photos and other trinkets that share information about your child.

Why use a scrapbook to help with meeting unfamiliar relatives?
Using a scrapbook is an easy, fun, and creative tool that provides opportunities for your child to share with family members by communicating through photos. Some children may need more time to process what is being said, photos provide an additional prompt.

How to use a scrapbook
1. Make a list of people, places, events, and objects that are important to your child.
2. Take photos of people, places, events, and objects that are important to your child.
3. Print off photos and decide upon pictures to include in scrapbook.
4. Discuss the photos.

What to do before vacation
1. Make a list of people, places, events, and objects that are important to your child. Discuss with your child that he will be meeting relatives for the first time. Make sure to explain that these unfamiliar relatives do not know a lot about him. To help your child share details about his life, explain that together you will be taking photos and then create a scrapbook.
2. Take photos of the items on the list. Your child may be able to take the pictures by himself, or with your guidance. Discuss with your child how he can take the photos; your child can point out objects and have you take the photos, or you can take turns taking photos. Provide some examples of different ways he can be involved; not every child can hold a camera and take pictures.
3. Print the photos and ask your child to pick his favorite ones for the scrapbook. Obtain a small photo album that reflects your child's personality and style. Choose something that will be easy to bring with on vacation. Help your child arrange the photos in the album. Your child can also decorate the scrapbook with stickers or his own artwork. You or your child might add captions under each photo. This may help unfamiliar relatives understand the photo and better interact with your child.
   For a high tech version of a scrapbook, use a digital camera to take and upload photos to programs such as Snapfish or Shutterfly (www.snapfish.com or www.shutterfly.com). You

and your child can digitally format a scrapbook and have it professionally printed, which will be mailed, directly to your home. You can also have a copy sent to your relatives. If your child has a visual impairment you can create an auditory scrapbook recording his voice describing each of the people, places events identified in step 2. Praise his involvement.

4. Discuss the photos with his siblings, speech therapist, and/ or teacher to help prepare him for talking about the photos with relatives. You can prompt your child with questions. Think about the kinds of questions an unfamiliar relative might ask your child. Questions might include:
   - What is going on in this photo?
   - Why did you take photos of these places?
   - Who is this?
   - Why did you choose these specific photos?

What to do on vacation
- Take the scrapbook you made at home on vacation.
- Encourage your child to share his scrapbook with family members.

What to do after vacation
- At home, print the photos your child took on vacation and add them to the scrapbook. Then your child can use the scrapbook to share with local family, friends, and teachers.

Travel Concern - Sharing with Peers on Vacation
Intervention Strategy - Cartoon

Peer interaction is a concern for many children with special needs. On vacation your child may need to interact with new peers when he participates in children's programs at a resort, on a cruise or when visiting family or friends with children. There are many social skills that are relevant to interacting with peers and many strategies you can use to prepare your child and teach social interaction skills. In this section we will focus on peer interaction skills to enable your child to successfully participate in children's activities on vacation. A child who shares has more positive relationships with their peers. To begin to teach your child to share we will use a **cartoon.**

What is a cartoon?

A cartoon is an illustration of an interaction between 2 or more people, incorporating the use of speech bubbles describing what other people think, do, or say. Although cartooning has limited scientific verification, some evidence suggests children with autism spectrum disorders may benefit from using cartooning to interpret social situations. Carol Gray developed one type of cartooning strategy known as Comic Strip Conversations (Gray, 1994).

Why use a cartoon to help teach sharing with a peer?

Cartoons can illustrate the behavior in which your child should engage. Cartoons can also show your child's thoughts and feelings about sharing with peers and help your child figure out what to do in social situations.

How to use a cartoon

1. Identify desired behavior.
2. Create a cartoon.
3. Review the cartoon and role-play.
4. Practice the skill in a real life setting.

What to do before vacation

1. Identify skill - *Sharing with peers*
2. Create a cartoon.
   It can be as simple as using blank unlined paper with simple drawings such as stick figures, to computer generated figures. If possible include your child's input in the process. Reinforce your child's attempts. Before you create your cartoon you need to look at your vacation and think of a scenario

when you child will be in the company of a peer. If your child is in a children's program chances are they are going to be required to share a toy.

- Identify the setting - children's program on a cruise ship.
- Decide on the plot and interaction required – sharing a toy with a peer.
- Draw pictures that represent the plot. Use facial expressions to represent emotions.
- Write the cartoon in dialogue form. Use conversation bubbles to identify conversation between the two children. Begin the cartoon with a greeting. For example, "Hi, my name is Billy."
- Identify thoughts by using thought bubbles. For example, "Gee, I was really mean to Billy and made him sad."
- Include a solution. Use conversation or thought bubbles.

3. Review the cartoon and role-play. Discuss with your child that he may have to share with other children while on vacation. Read the cartoon with your child. Act out the situation in the cartoon to role-play and practice sharing.
4. Practice the skill of sharing a toy in a real life setting such as at a friend's house or playground. Review the cartoon and then have your child practice sharing a toy with a sibling or peer.

What to do on vacation
- Bring the cartoon with you on vacation.
- Read the cartoon with your child before he is to share with other children.
- Create a cartoon with your child for other social interactions.
- Provide reinforcers when your child shares.

Chan, a 5 year old boy with Down syndrome, is going on a cruise to the Bahamas with his family. His parents would like to put Chan in the children's program for a few hours a day for social interaction and to give them a bit of respite time; however, Chan's parents are concerned that he will have difficulty sharing toys with other children. Chan started kindergarten this year and his teacher has noted that Chan has difficulty sharing with others. Since Chan likes cartoons, his parents decided to use this strategy to teach sharing. Chan's parents checked the Web site for the cruise line to identify activities and games that Chan would be likely to engage in at the children's program. They wrote several cartoons, each for a different activity. Each cartoon illustrated sharing. Prior to vacation Chan's parents will read the script with him everyday before he leaves for school. Chan's mother will send a copy of the script to school and encourage his teacher to review with him before playtime.

STAYING SAFE

Safety is always a big concern. Concerns are intensified when a child has special needs and when traveling. A child with an autism spectrum disorder may have communication difficulties and behavioral challenges that affect his safety. A child with an attention deficit hyperactivity disorder may be highly active, impulsive, and inattentive. He may end up in an unsafe situation because he is not paying attention to obstacles in his way. A child with a developmental or cognitive impairment may not have learned how to recognize dangerous situations or what to do to keep safe. A child who has a visual impairment, is deaf or hard of hearing, or has a physical challenge may have difficulty navigating the new environment and anticipating upcoming dangers. Ensuring safety while traveling requires identifying safety rules and teaching those rules to your child. In this section, we discuss special considerations related to wandering - an all too common problem for learners with special needs.

To prepare your child for vacation, begin teaching your child about safety well in advance of your trip. Think about where you will be going and what you will be doing on vacation. Consider any new experiences that your child will encounter on vacation and concentrate on safety rules that will apply to these new situations. When teaching safety, take into consideration your child's cognitive abilities, his age, strengths, skills, and personal interests to build on his knowledge base.

Teach Safety

Step 1	**Identify Safety Rules**
Step 2	**Teach Your Child Safety Rules**
Step 3	**Reinforce Safety Rules Using Interactive Activities**

Step 1 Identify Safety Rules

Identify the safety rules you need to address with your child. Phrase rules in terms of what your child should do and be sure to consider your child's abilities and age. The rules you identify will reflect where you are traveling. If you are visiting a big city, you will need to identify safety rules for walking on the sidewalk and crossing the street. If you are taking a cruise focus on safety when navigating on and off ramps, steep stairs, staying off the balcony railings, and behavior in the children's program. Focus on water safety rules if the resort where you are staying has a pool. Write your rules on the "Family Safety Rules" worksheet.

"Family Safety Rules"

◆ Example: "I will hold my mommy's hand when we cross the street."

◆ _____

◆ _____

◆ _____

◆ _____

Step 2 Teach Safety Rules

Identify the vacation activities that will be relevant for your trip. Add to and modify the rules for each scenario to reflect the rules that you created for your child.

- Use the following scenarios to begin to discuss safety rules with your child. The illustrations show Jamie and his mother engaging in various vacation activities that require safe behavior.
- Look at the pictures with your child. Read the rules with your child and ask questions about the pictures.
- Model the safety rules related to the scenarios. Role-play the different scenarios to practice safe behavior.

Safety Rules Around the Streets

☆ Hold parents hand at all times.

☆ Walk on the sidewalk.

☆ Stop at the curb.

☆ Use crosswalks.

☆ Wait for the "walk" signal and green light when crossing the street.

☆ Stop if I hear a siren.

☆ Stop, look left, look right, and then left again before crossing.

☆ Watch for turning vehicles.

☆ Never cross the street between parked cars.

☆ Be extra careful when walking by a driveway.

☆ Tell an adult if I need help getting something from the street (e.g. ball or toy that rolls into the road).

Safety Rules at the Airport

☆ Stay close to my parent at all times.

☆ Hold my parents hand at all times.

☆ Stand behind my parent when near the luggage machine.

☆ Be extra careful around sliding doors, revolving doors, and automatic doors.

☆ Always stay where mommy can see me.

☆ Watch for luggage carts and golf carts transporting passengers.

☆ Go to the bathroom with mommy or daddy.

☆ Follow parent's instructions when going through airport security. For example, when going through airport security, my parent will go through first, then I will go, then my older sibling, parent or relative will go.

Safety Rules at Attractions

☆ Always hold my parent's hand.

☆ Stay with my parents at all times.

☆ Walk. Do not run.

☆ Stay off railing at the zoo.

☆ Do not feed the animals.

☆ Keep my hands and body away from the animals.

☆ Stay away from the water at aquariums.

☆ Remember keep arms and legs inside the ride.

☆ Stay on the ride until the operator says it is okay to stand up and get off.

☆ Wear personal identification and know its location.

☆ Go to the bathroom with my mommy or daddy.

Safety Rules Around Water

☆ Swim only with an adult present.

☆ Follow all posted safety rules.

☆ Keep hands to myself (no pushing, shoving).

☆ Walk around pool.

☆ Dive only in areas that are clearly marked for diving.

☆ Keep out of water if there is lightning.

☆ Drink plenty of water to prevent dehydration.

☆ Wear sunscreen, sunglasses, hats and protective clothing.

☆ Contact a lifeguard if I need help.

☆ Swim only in designated safe areas of oceans, rivers, or lakes.

☆ Wear a life jacket when boating and otherwise appropriate.

Safety Rules at Accommodations

☆ Keep the door locked at all times.

☆ Tell a grownup if someone knocks at the door.

☆ Sleep on the bed – do not jump.

☆ Sit on chairs – do not climb.

☆ Stay off railings.

☆ Keep my hands by my side when around doorjambs and elevator doors.

☆ Press the emergency button if stuck in an elevator.

☆ Carefully walk onto the escalator and hold the rail.

☆ Use luggage carts for luggage only – not for riding.

☆ Remember that television stands can tip over if I climb on them or pull on them.

☆ Stay away from electrical outlets.

Safety Rules When Lost

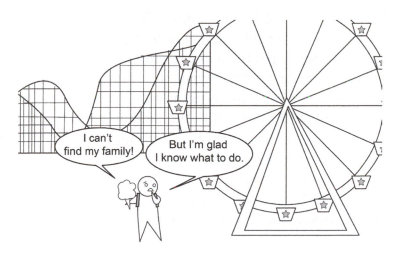

★ Stay where I am.

★ Go to the designated place to meet my family and wait (for older children).

★ While I am waiting I will look for a uniformed police officer, security guard, store/business personnel wearing a nametag, cashier, ticket booth employee, or a mommy with a child and tell them, "I am lost."

★ Show the police officer or employee my identification information.

★ Dial 9-1-1 for help if I can see a telephone.

★ Always stay at the attraction and never go to the parking lot without my parent.

Step 3 Reinforce Safety Rules Using Interactive Activities

After you teach your child safety rules, reinforce the rule on a regular basis. Look for teachable moments to reinforce safety rules so your child will know what to do in a real life setting. For example, if you are at the shopping mall with your child and you see an unhappy child run away from his parent, point out the dangers of running away. Brainstorm with your child what he should do instead of running away if he were unhappy. Provide appropriate alternative ways to handle being upset. Stress that running away is never an option.

Use the following interactive activities, "Who Am I and Where Would You See Me?" "Pick the Safe Picture," "What Should You Do?" and "Safety Crossing the Street" to reinforce safety rules.

"Who Am I and Where Would You See Me?"

Your child will encounter many different people while traveling. The different professionals are often important to help keep your child safe. For example, the captain on the airplane provides important instructions especially if there is a problem; hotel staff can help your child if he is lost.

Goal: Child will be able to identify professionals and where he might see them on vacation.

Materials: Index cards, glue, markers, and photos or pictures of different professions that your child may encounter on vacation.

1. With your child, discuss the different professionals with whom he will likely come into contact while traveling. For example, at the airport your child will see security personnel, sales agents, baggage handlers, and crewmembers. Focus on those who are most likely to be relevant to helping your child stay safe.
2. Discuss prior knowledge your child may have about the people he will see when traveling. For example, if your child has taken a trip on a train, ask him if he remembers meeting the conductor.
3. Obtain pictures of the professionals from Web sites, clip art, magazines, coloring books, old catalogs, and/or newspapers. Below is a list of professions your child may meet on vacation.
4. Adhere the picture of one profession on each index card.
5. Hold up one picture so your child can see it and ask, "Who Am I and Where Would You See Me?" Provide prompts if needed.
   For example:

- Who am I? *Ship captain* --- Where would you see me? *On the ship.*
- Who am I? *Doctor* --- Where would you see me? *On a cruise, in a hospital, in an office.*
- Who am I? *Nurse* --- Where would you see me? *In a doctor's office, in a hospital, in a medical center.*
- Who am I? *Waitress/waiter* --- Where would you see me? *In a restaurant, diner, place that serves food.*
- Who am I? *Housekeeper* --- Where would you see me? *In a hotel, motel, resort.*
- Who am I? *Pilot* --- Where would you see me? *On an airplane, walking through an airport.*
- Who am I? *Chef or cook* --- Where would you see me? *At a restaurant.*

- Who am I? *Front desk employee* --- Where would you see me? *At a hotel, motel, resort.*
- Who am I? *Bellhop* --- *Where* would you see me? *At a hotel, motel, resort.*
- Who am I? *Crew attendant* --- Where would you see me? *On a ship or boat.*
- Who am I? *Childcare worker* --- Where would you see me? *In a children's program.*
- Who am I? *Salesperson* --- *Where* would you see me? *In a store.*
- Who am I? *Ticket agent* --- Where would you see me? *At an attraction selling tickets.*
- Who am I? *Zookeeper* --- Where would you see me? *At the zoo.*
- Who am I? *Park Ranger* --- Where would you see me? *At the beach, park.*
- Who am I? *Lifeguard* --- Where would you see me? *At the pool, beach, lake.*
- Who am I? *Taxi driver* --- Where would you see me? *Driving a car in a city.*
- Who am I? *Conductor* --- Where would you see me? *On the train, in the train station.*
- Who am I? *Bus driver* --- Where would you see me? *On the bus, in the bus station.*
- Who am I? *Doorman* --- Where would you see me? *At the hotel, resort.*
- Who am I? *Security guard or police officer* --- Where would you see me? *At attractions, on the street, in banks, in shopping malls, stores.*

Continue the fun on vacation!

Create a list of all the professionals your child may see on vacation. Challenge your child to a scavenger hunt to find all the different professionals. Every time your child sees one of the professionals on his list, he can check it off. This can be a fun game for the entire family. Reward the winners!

Activity Modifications
If your child is nonverbal, he may be able to use another mode of communication (e.g., sign language) to answer the questions. Alternatively, place two pictures on a table. Have your child point to the picture. For children with visual impairments, you can adapt this activity by providing your child with a detailed description of the person's job responsibilities. For example, say to your child, "When we are on the airplane, this person will welcome us on the plane, give us safety instructions, and bring us snacks, beverages, and a blanket. Who is this? "

"Pick the Safe Picture"

Goal: Child will be able to identify safe behavior that follows family safety rules.

Materials: Photos of safe and unsafe behavior for your family's safety rules.

1. Use the illustrations provided here and/or create your own using photos, drawings, and/or clip art.
2. Show your child the pictures from one of the scenarios on the following pages. Either you or your child should read the description of the scenario.
3. Ask your child which picture shows safe behavior and which picture does not. Your child can circle the picture in which the child is following safety rules. You might also ask follow-up questions:
   - What rules is Jamie following to stay safe when crossing the street?
   - Why is it important to follow these safety rules when crossing the street?

Scenario 1

Jamie is on vacation with his parents in New York City. They are spending the day exploring the city. Jamie will have to cross many streets throughout the day to get from one attraction to another. Circle the picture in which Jamie is following safety rules.

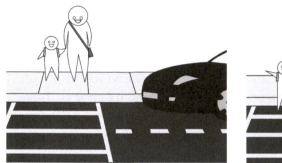 

Scenario 2

Jamie and his family are returning from their trip to California. After departing from the airplane, Jamie and his family need to go to the luggage carousel to retrieve their bags. Jamie is excited when he sees his luggage on the carousel. Circle the picture in which Jamie is following safety rules.

Scenario 3

Jamie is at the zoo with his family. He is very excited to see the tigers, lions, monkey, bears, elephants, and giraffes. Circle the picture in which Jamie is following safety rules.

Scenario 4

Jamie is at the hotel pool with his family. He is very excited to swim in the pool. Circle the picture in which Jamie is following safety rules.

Scenario 5

Jamie is staying in a hotel in Florida with his family. He and his mother are in their hotel room. His mother is in the bathroom when someone knocks on the door. Circle the picture in which Jamie is following safety rules.

"What Should You Do?"

Goal: Child will be able to identify a safe solution to a safety problem.

Materials: Index cards, markers

1. Based on the rules you taught your child, create scenarios and "What Should You Do?" questions. These scenarios should focus on a potentially dangerous situation. Ask your child to problem solve the situations to help learn and reinforce safe behavior. You can pair the questions with pictures of unsafe situations and even role-play. Modify the questions to meet your child's needs.
   Examples of questions:

   - What should you do if you want to play in the pool at the hotel and your parents are busy unpacking?
   - What should you do if your ball rolls into the pool?

- What should you do if you are on a ride at an amusement park and the flashing lights are bothering you?
- What should you do if you cannot find your parents when you are at the museum?
- What should you do if you want to see the elephants, but your family is feeding the ducks at the zoo?
- What should you do if people in a crowd bother you?
- What should you do if you need a break and want to be by yourself?
- What should you do if your mom says, "Stop?"

2. Describe a scenario (and present pictures or role-play the scenario) and ask your child, "What Should You Do?" If you child has difficulty responding with a safe solution, provide suggestions. Present a few options so your child can pick.
3. Reinforce your child's participation and correct responses about safe behavior.

Additional activities

- Make doubles of the cards and have your child match professions; your child could group people by where he's likely to see them (e.g., all the amusement park workers; the hotel workers, staff on a cruise).
- Older children can write a story about one of the professionals and where he would come in contact with this person.

"Safety Crossing the Street"

Goal: Child will be able to safely walk across the street.

Materials: Masking tape (or chalk), coin or toy

1. Discuss with your child the rules you identified for crossing the street and street dangers.

2. Create a virtual road and sidewalk in your driveway using masking tape or drawing an outline of a street in chalk.
3. Practice walking on the sidewalk and crossing the street following the rules you identified for your family. For example, practice stopping at the curb; have your child practice holding your hand. This is a good time to also practice following critical safety instructions such as stopping when you say, "Stop" or "Freeze." Practice them often and use these key words in various situations with your child until you are confident that he will comply with your directive.
4. To practice rules about running into the street and getting a grown up to help if a toy is in the street, place a coin or toy in the middle of the virtual street. Practice what your child should do.
5. Once your child shows safe behavior near the virtual street in the driveway, take a walk with your child to practice street safety.

Depending upon your child's age, you might promote independent safe walking by giving your child opportunities to walk a little bit ahead of you. Before you let go of your child's hand remind him when you say, "Stop," he must stop. When you say, "Go," he may begin to walk ahead again.

Safety Precautions: Wandering

Many parents are reluctant to travel for fear their child will wander off when traveling. Wandering is a significant safety concern at home and also when traveling. (Anderson, Law, Daniel, Rice, Mandell, Hagopian 2012) found that roughly half of children with ASD wander or bolt and more than half of these children go missing. These statistics are alarming. When planning your trip, consider the following safety precautions:

- Think about how you can restructure the environment so your child is less likely to wander. You may want to secure your child's hotel room/cabin by installing battery-operated alarms on doors and windows. Check with your hotel or cruise line if safety alarms are available for your room or cabin. If they are not available, you can purchase them before leaving home at Walmart or Radio Shack. According to the National Autism Association, Guardian Lock is a portable lock that you can use when traveling. To locate the Guardian Lock online, Google "Guardian Lock Autism" and the first hit provides a link to the lock along with a YouTube video. You might add prompts in the hotel room to remind your child about safe behavior. For example, place a "Stop" sign on the room door to remind your child that he is not permitted to leave without permission.

- Notify the staff at the hotel or on the ship that your child is prone to wandering and to contact you immediately if he is seen anywhere without an approved adult. Introduce all adults that may be with your child to the staff and leave your cell phone number with them to contact you if your child is seen wandering. If you provide staff with an information card about your child and his disability, include your cell number on the card.

- Book a room away from the swimming pool if your child tends to wander and loves to swim. You may want to consider purchasing the Turtle, a wristband that locks and sounds an alarm if it is immersed in water.

- Obtain a tracking device to aid with locating your child if he wanders away from you. Tracking devices are worn on the wrist/ankle to locate your child through radio frequency. Check with law enforcement for information about Project Lifesaver (www.projectlifesaver.org) or LoJack SafetyNet (www.safetynetbylojack.com). For additional types of tracking technology visit the http://awaare.org. Cell phones may be equipped with a global positioning system (GPS). If your child carries a cell phone or if you are comfortable providing him with one, GPS may be another way to locate your child if he wanders.

- Wear identification to ensure your child can share important information with people who can help him. There are many identification options on the market. Identification should be discrete and include your child's name, parents' names, hotel/cruise, address, telephone number, and any important information such as health/ medical/allergies. Include a card with a description of your child's disability and how to best interact with him. If you are traveling in a foreign county, make sure information on your child's identification is written in both English and the language of the country you are visiting. Create and bring extras of your child's identification in case one is misplaced. Discrete identification can be:

  - Bracelets that are colorful and fun to wear
  - Stickers that stick to the inside of the shoe
  - Velcro shoe ID labels
  - Wallet ID cards
  - ID card pinned inside child's clothing
  - Temporary tattoo (safetytat.com, tattooswithapurpose. com)
  - Necklaces

- The Federal Bureau of Investigation Child ID App is a free tool for parents giving them an easy way to electronically store pictures and vital information about their child in case of an emergency. The app also includes tips on keeping children safe and guidance if a child goes missing. The app is available for I-Phone (http://itunes.apple.com/us/app/ fbi-child-id/id446158585) & Android Operating systems.

- Check out The National Autism Association's Big Red Safety Toolkit for more helpful information. The Toolkit includes statistics, resources, and checklists, emergency information forms for the community and first responders, types of tracking devices, and sample social stories, as well as suggestions about securing your home. You can download The Big Red Safety Toolkit at http://awaare.org.

- To protect your child's identity avoid wearing any items that contain your child's name. The National Center for Missing and Exploited Children suggests that a potential abductor can use such identifying information to gain your child's trust.

- To help spot your child in a crowd and help your child spot you, have everyone in the entire family wear the same brightly colored shirts (if you can't find the same colored shirts think about dyeing white-tee shirts all the same color).

- If your child is missing, your first call should be to the law enforcement entity or agency. You can also make a report to NCMEC at 1-800-THE-LOST.

Important Information

Accidental drowning is a serious safety concern for parents. Since many families choose to take beach vacations or stay at a hotel with a pool, it is extremely important that your child learn water safety. Review water safety with your child prior to and while on vacation. Consider viewing videos about water safety and even participating in some of the water safety web based activities. Some websites to get you started: http://water.epa.gov/learn/kids/beachkids/games.cfm, Bobber The Water Safety Dog: www.bobber.info Teaching your child how to swim is a necessity. If your child does not know how to swim, be sure to keep him safe by wearing a floatation device at all times around water. Actively supervise your child around water regardless of his swimming skills.

Remember to continue to follow safety rules on vacation. Safety experts stress the importance of parents/caregivers keeping their eye on their children at all times. Identification and tracking devices do not take the place of parents actively watching their children. Teaching safety rules, reviewing them and practicing them often are crucial for your child's safety. Safety does not take vacation when you are on vacation.

Supplementary Safety Information

To familiarize your child with important signs (i.e. exit, danger, stop, go, caution, no swimming, no diving, do not enter, slippery when wet) create signs and hang them around your house or in your backyard. For example, put a stop sign on the inside of your front door so your child knows that he must stop and talk to you before leaving the house or if you have a pool you can hang a sign saying no diving, no running and do not swim without supervision.

At amusement parks, carnivals, theme parks, accompany young children on rides, or if they are riding alone, be sure to wait with them in line, watch them enter the ride and immediately meet them when they exit the ride.

Plan ahead of time what your child should do if he becomes separated or lost from you. Make sure your child can provide his full name, address, telephone number (cell phone if traveling), and parent's name and knows where their ID (i.e. bracelet, shoe, necklace) is located.

Give older children a cell phone. Many cell phones are global position system enabled, making it possible for police to locate your child using the cell phone signal. You may not be able to hear your phone in a noisy area, use vibrate mode and put it in your pocket. For a child who is deaf or hard of hearing, be sure they know how to make a collect call on the TTY or TDD and say or type they need help.

Kids.gov is an informative U.S. Government official web portal for kids offering games, information on social studies, math, history, science, health, safety, and online safety.

According to The National Center for Missing & Exploited Children (NCMEC) one of the most important tools for law enforcers if your child is missing is an up-to-date picture of your child. The photo should be a recent color image of your child's head and shoulders. Hard copies are good, but an electronic version of the photo is preferred. The photo should be updated every six months for children 6 years or younger and then every year after that or when your child's appearance changes. While on vacation you might take a photo of your child at the beginning of each day. This will guarantee that you have the most recent photo of your child readily available should you need to show it to authorities. For more important safety information visit www.ncmec.org.

If your child has a visual impairment, The National Center for Missing & Exploited Children has compiled a number of informational brochures on teen and child safety into one Braille book offered through National Braille Press (NBP). A free version of the brochure in Braille can be obtained by calling 1-888-965-8965.

Once reunited with your child speak with them in a calm reassuring manner. Do not be angry with him about getting lost – he will probably be frightened and need comfort.

What to do next?

Now that you have planned your trip, secured any special provisions required, and addressed your child's travel concerns following our Three Step method you are ready to move on to Departure.

Questions and Answers

Q. My 6 year old child with ASD has difficulty sitting still is there anything I can do to help him be more patient on the airplane?

A. Yes, before your trip, have you child pretend he is on an airplane sitting still and waiting for take-off. Start with a small number of minutes (begin with a number that you know your child can accomplish with success). Increase the amount of time gradually. You will need to practice this activity prior to going to the airport over a period of time. Add reinforcers for sitting quietly on the plane, using Behavioral Specific Praise Statements.

Q. My child is 10 years old and diagnosed with Asperger's syndrome. He is often reluctant to do anything we suggest on vacation. Is there a strategy I can use to encourage compliance?

A. Give your child a choice of 2 or 3 activities to choose from that you know he will like. Let him pick 1 activity. Giving choices will help your child feel empowered and more in control. Remember to give choices that you allow.

Working with high school students, I often incorporated choice making and encouragement to obtain positive results. For example: *"I worked with CM a 15 year old diagnosed with an Anxiety Disorder, ADHD and School Phobia. CM often experienced difficulty getting out of his parent's car to enter the building in the morning. He expressed anxiety about going to his classroom prior to early morning announcements. I gave CM the option of sitting in my office until morning announcements were over or to sit in our conference room to work on his classwork during that time. CM understood his two choices and that I would be supportive of his choice. I prompted him to choose and reinforced his choice. I have found choice-making to be a highly effective strategy. This strategy worked with CM." –J.J.*

Q. My 9 year old daughter is sensory sensitive and wants to go to a theme park. What can I do to help her?

A. Depending on the severity of your daughter's sensory issues, precautions need to be put into place to help her with the loud noises, crowds, and bright lights. We have found the following interventions to be effective for children with sensory sensitivities:

- Contact the theme park for a list of rides and their sensory ratings. Avoid rides that have a lot of visual and auditory input.
- Prepare your child by creating a visual story ahead of time to familiarize her with the park.
- Teach her relaxation techniques.
- Go off-season. Peak season is crowded.
- Bring earplugs, headphones, and sunglasses.

Q. While on vacation, I want to take my son on a day trip that requires us to be on a tour bus for several hours. When bored, he can become aggressive and tantrum. What can I do to prevent this?

A. Keep your son busy to avoid boredom. One way is to get him excited about the trip. You can do this by giving him a book/visual story/brochure to look at and discuss. You can also re-direct inappropriate behaviors – use distracters to take your child's mind off the long bus ride. Redirect your child's focus to something else, reading, listening to music on his iPod, playing a hand held video game, coloring, drawing, and writing in a journal. You can also:

- Ask a question about something you know he likes or hand him a favorite item. This usually will help re-direct a child.
- Teach progressive relaxation and breathing techniques to reduce anxiety.
- Take advantage of breaks, get out of the bus, walk around, and stretch whenever possible.

On the way home, you can look at your postcards, souvenirs, and photos on your digital camera, which will help the time pass quickly.

"Over the years I taught many aggressive students. One of my students had a tendency to overreact and initiate fights. I learned from expe-

rience that calling her name and asking her to stop just riled her up even more. I decided to try something new. I had left over Valentine's Day heart pencils in my desk draw. When I saw her frustration building, I would walk to her desk and give her a heart pencil. This calmed her down completely. I told her to feel the love and think positive. This type of re-directing can work anywhere. Helping your child shift their thoughts away from what is frustrating them is the key to redirection."
–I.K.

Q. My child has sensory sensitivities; crowded areas, loud noises, certain textures and bright lights bother her. Is it possible for us to take vacation?

A. Yes, going on vacation may be a bit of a challenge depending on where you are planning to go. If you are planning to go to a theme or amusement park, you may be able to secure a Guest Assistance Pass for your child. This will allow you access to a priority line with fewer people and speed up the waiting process. You will need to obtain a note from your child's physician stating her diagnosis to obtain a pass. Teach your child about her sensitivities – let her know it is okay to ask for space and to remove herself from an over stimulated setting to regroup with your permission. Sunglasses, earphones and packing your child's sheets and blankets are also advisable.

Q. My child, Joey is diagnosed with autism. We are planning a trip next summer. How can I help him generalize skills when we go on vacation?

A. We think Temple Grandin said it simply and best:

"To help a child generalize a skill it must be taught in many different settings. If you only choose one setting the child may think that the rule only applies to one specific setting" (Grandin, 2002).

Many children with autism have difficulty generalizing skills across different settings (e.g. home, school, and in the community). Skills demonstrated in one setting are not automatically transferred to other settings. Generalization takes time. Be patient. When your child learns one way of understanding something, teach another way of saying the same thing, and occasionally use the old one, eventually introducing different ways of saying the same thing. The goal is that your child is able to respond appropriately when stated in different words that mean the same thing.

Provide different models, such as parents, grandparents, siblings, aunts, uncles, and friends, to teach your child desired skills. Inform your child's teacher that you are planning to take your child on vacation. Request that generalization is practiced during the day with different people e.g. teachers, aides, speech and language therapist, occupational therapist, and case managers in a variety of settings e.g. classroom, cafeteria, in the hallways and offices to give your child the opportunity to generalize skills with different people in different settings. Practice and more practice will help generalize skills.

*A good plan is like a road map: it shows the final destination
and usually the best way to get there.
-- H. Stanley Judd*

DEPARTURE
TRAVEL ESSENTIALS

READY, SET, GO!

In this chapter you will find a timeline to guide you in planning for your vacation. A travel-packing checklist is provided to make sure you are prepared and have all the essentials needed before leaving home.

Book your trip as soon as possible. Many people wait for that last minute deal, however, we do not recommend this – especially if you need to put in place special provisions for your child. When you are planning a trip with a family member that requires special provisions and supports, the more time you give yourself the better.

We have included a suggested timeline to act as a guide for you to plan and prepare for vacation.

Planning Timeline

Six Months - Year

Determine your budget
What is your budget for the vacation? How much do you want to spend for your vacation, and how much money will you need while you're away. There may be added expenses when traveling with a child with special needs. See "additional costs" on your budget worksheet in Appendix 5.

Complete your "Family Interest Planner"
Complete the "Family Interest Planner" in Chapter 1.

Research destination

Contact state and local tourism office and request brochures. Most brochures will include a calendar of events and information about your destination. Read travel books and check out online resources to learn more about your destination. A travel consultant can be a valuable resource and possibly save you money.

Book transportation and accommodations

At the time of booking you may be required to pay a deposit for lodging accommodations. Airfare needs to be paid in full at time of booking.

Inquire what special provisions or services are available for your child. Refer back to the "Special Needs Pre-Trip Questionnaire" in Chapter 2. Refer to this questionnaire when speaking with your travel consultant or vacation provider to inform them of your child's special needs.

Determine necessary travel documents

Depending on your destination there may be specific documents required e.g. a passport, driver's license, visa or vaccinations. For additional information on documents necessary for traveling visit: www.travel.state.gov

If you are traveling outside of the U.S. all family members will need a passport. If this is your first time applying for a passport give enough time for processing. Check to make sure all passports are up to date. All passports must be valid through six months after your return date. This is a TSA requirement for all international travel. If any family member needs to renew or obtain a passport, book your travel start date taking into consideration the time it will take to receive your new documents.

To apply for a new passport or renew your original passport, a passport photo is needed. Passport photos can be taken at a variety of locations. To make the process less stressful for your child, choose a location that is familiar to your child, such as a local pharmacy. If your child is not accustomed to having his photo taken or has trouble with a camera flash, practice taking photos at home. You can apply for a passport at any passport offices or you can inquire at your local post office. For more information on how to apply for a passport visit www.usps.com.

Obtain necessary documentation if only one parent is traveling with your child outside the U.S. Children under the age of 18 not traveling with both of their legal guardians internationally must provide documentation to depart and enter the U.S. You will need two notarized copies – one when departing the country and one when you return to the U.S., documents include:

- Permission to Travel Letter in Appendix 6.
- Divorce and custody agreement if applicable.
- A certified copy of the death certificate if parent is deceased.

Inquire about travel insurance

Travel insurance is advisable for anyone taking a trip. Travel insurance is a protective policy to cover unforeseen emergencies when traveling. There are different types of travel insurance: trip cancellation, baggage insurance, emergency medical insurance, and accidental death insurance. Travel insurance can be purchased as a package or separately. Many options are available through the airline, cruise line, tour companies, or private travel insurance companies. Travel insurance will provide you with peace of mind if you need to cancel because of illness or unforeseen circumstance.

Teach vacation safety

To prepare your child for vacation, think about where you will be going and what you will be doing on vacation. Consider any new experience that your child will encounter on vacation and concentrate on safety rules that will apply to these new situations. Refer to Safety in Chapter 3 for activities, scenarios, and strategies to teach your child.

Begin practicing Dry Run strategies
Start the Dry Run strategies as soon as possible. This may mean collecting information and material from different sources to create your stories, cartoons, schedules, and/or video modeling. Purchase a calendar for your child to start the countdown. Start compiling items to be included in your child's Wait Box. It may not be possible to start this early, however, do the best you can.

Two - Three Months

Schedule medical appointments
Contact your child's physician to let him know about your travel plans. If your child is on medication, obtain an extra prescription in the event the medication is lost or misplaced. If you are traveling out of the U.S. the prescription must include the scientific name rather than the brand name of the medication. Some FDA-approved products have the same brand names as the U.S. products, but contain completely different active ingredients. For additional information and a list of "Identical U.S. and Foreign Brand Names Associated With Different Active Ingredients" refer to the FDA Public Health Advisory article, January 2006 at www.fda.gov/drugs.

Review vaccination history with your child's physician. Make sure all vaccinations are up to date before traveling. Check on what vaccinations are required when traveling to a foreign country. You may need to schedule an appointment with a travel medicine specialist, a person who is familiar with vaccine recommendations and disease alerts associated with international travel. Ask your physician for a referral. You can also find a directory of private travel clinics throughout the U.S. and abroad through the International Society of Travel Medicine –www.istm.org. For more information on private travel clinics throughout the U.S. contact the Center for Disease Control and Prevention at 1-800-232-4636 or www.cdc.gov/travel. Get the recommended vaccinations before you travel. Plan early since some vaccinations take up to 4 to 6 weeks to provide full protection.

Secure a note from your child's physician if:

- Medication is in liquid or syringe form, especially if liquid medication is over the allotted ounces allowed by airlines.
- Special equipment or medical supplies are necessary.
- A Guest Assistance pass for amusement parks or other attractions is needed.

Compose medical history

If you are traveling with a child who has a medical issue or severe allergy:

- Compose a brief medical history.
- Download medical history on 911 medical alert cards. See Appendix 3 for additional information.
- Contact your insurance company to make sure your family is covered when traveling to a different country. Some insurance companies only cover medical care within the United States.

Refill prescription medications

Refill all prescription medication. This is especially important if you mail order your child's medication or the medication is difficult to obtain. To board a plane, liquid medications have to meet TSA regulations, the three-ounce rule, meaning they must be in three-ounce-or-less containers (not four-ounce containers with three ounces of medicine). If your liquid medication exceeds this amount, bring a physicians note explaining why more medication is needed.

Arrange any special medical supplies/equipment

Arrange for any special medical supplies or equipment that your child will need on vacation. Request an email confirmation for your records to take with you on your trip. The resources given in Appendix 3 provide you with a sample of the names, addresses, and phone numbers of local hospital, pharmacies, and medical supply stores in the area of your destination within and out of the U.S. Most medical supply stores will deliver equipment and supplies to your vacation site. The resources given are a sample of the many providers. For specific information about having medical supplies or equipment delivered to your hotel or cruise ship, refer to Chapter 2.

Secure identification system

Secure identification for your child. There are a variety of methods on the market. You can use an ID bracelet, clothing with identification markings, or non-permanent tattoos. High tech systems, such as GPS tracking watches are available through electronic companies giving you real time positional information about your child. For more information refer to Safety in Chapter 3.

Research and finalize the attractions to visit

Research and finalize the attractions and activities you will visit on your vacation. Check the Web sites for hours of operation and admission. You may also be able to download a map of the attraction prior to your visit.

Rent a car

- Book early. If you require a wheelchair accessible van contact rental companies that provide this type of vehicle. Request an email confirmation for your records. A list of companies can be found in Appendix 3.
- When deciding on the size of the car, consider: space for luggage, special equipment, the comfort needs of your family, and your budget.
- Whenever possible select a car or van you are familiar with driving, as each model may operate differently.

Arrange for kennel

Arrange for kenneling or other pet care. Some kennels may have vaccination requirements. You may need to make an appointment with your vet if your pet's vaccinations are not up to date.

Make final payments

Make final payments on your lodging or cruise. Failure to submit the balance due on time may result in the cancellation of your reservation. Check with your travel consultant or vacation provider about payment guidelines.

One Month

Start thinking about packing

Think about where you will be going, what you will be doing, and the weather. You can check the weather for your destination by visiting www.weatherchannel.com and typing in your destination. Plan out clothing and shoes you will need for these activities. This might include bathing suits, special shoes, hats, and sports equipment. Will you need dressy attire? If you are going on a cruise, check on the dress code, as there may be a night when you will be required to wear formal attire. Have all members of your family try on their clothes to make sure they fit. If you need to purchase additional apparel, shop now. You do not want to be visiting the mall the day before your trip. Refer to the Travel Packing Checklist at the end of this chapter.

Schedule transportation to airport

If you are not driving to the airport, schedule transportation. You can use a shuttle service or private car service. If you have a small child reserve a car seat when booking.

One - Two Weeks

Notify

- Credit card companies that you will be traveling to another state or country to prevent restriction on your credit card. With the increase of identity theft, credit card companies are denying access to credit card charges outside your general area at home unless notified in advance.
- Mail and newspaper providers to stop delivery

- Cell phone provider when traveling out of the U.S. to discuss options/plans that may be put in place so you can make and receive phone calls.

Confirm

- Hotel, car rental, lodging, and air reservations with your travel provider.
- Special provisions, equipment, and devices needed with the company or vacation provider. Request an email confirmation for your records and take a copy with you on your vacation.

Pack suitcases

- Refer to the Travel Packing Checklist at the end of this chapter.
- Select clothing that does not wrinkle. Keep similar color themes and mix and match. Check if you have access to laundry services. If so, you can take fewer pieces of clothing.
- Rolling clothes and using travel compressors save space and allows small items to fit into the corners of your suitcase. Use plastic bags for shoes to avoid soiling clothing and put socks and other small items in shoes to save space.
- Place all toiletries in plastic bags to avoid spills, and put them all in one suitcase for easy access.
- Give your child his own suitcase and have him pack for himself. Refer to the "choice making" activity in Chapter 3. When packing put your child's clothing in the order they will need to put on while dressing. For example, top to bottom – place underwear, shirt, pants, and socks together and tie each outfit with a ribbon to secure.

Pack Fun Bag

You will need to prepare your child's fun bag ahead of time. Include items your child will like. Let him help you choose items for his bag. The contents will differ depending on the age and needs of your child. Most children like the following: snacks, sensory toys, puzzle books, audio books, magnetic drawing devices, special comfort items, earplugs, headsets, audio-visual items, crayon, pencils and drawing pads.

Don't forget to buy yourself something special, a new bathing suit, beach cover up, shoes, an outfit, a bestseller book, and schedule a manicure/pedicure.

Day Before

Print out boarding passes and confirmations for the hotel/cruise, travel insurance policies, medical supplies, special equipment, and/or car and van rental.

Make copies of your passports, license, and all credits cards you will be using on the trip. Give your neighbors or family members your travel information. Carry an additional copy with you and store in a safe place.

Day of Travel

Lock all door and windows

Check stove, oven, and iron

Set timer on lights

Reduce heat, hot water heater, and A/C settings

Unplug appliances

Water plants

Set security alarm

Be sure your child has identification on him

Travel Packing Checklist

Travel documents
- [ ] Identification – passport, driver's license, visas, birth certificate
- [ ] Flight itinerary/boarding pass
- [ ] Hotel/cruise ship confirmation
- [ ] Rental car confirmation
- [ ] Travel insurance
- [ ] Medical/dental insurance cards
- [ ] Emergency phone numbers: physicians, family members, neighbors
- [ ] Notarized "Permission to Travel Letter" (one parent traveling with child)
- [ ] _____
- [ ] _____

Medical supplies/equipment
- [ ] First aid kit
- [ ] Car seat
- [ ] Portable motion detector alarm system
- [ ] CARES seat belt
- [ ] Airplane seat sheet
- [ ] Wheelchair/scooter/ charger
- [ ] Extension cord
- [ ] Walker
- [ ] Oxygen
- [ ] White cane
- [ ] Hearing aid/extra tubing/batteries
- [ ] Portable dehumidifier
- [ ] Dry pouch
- [ ] _____
- [ ] _____

Prescriptions/health
- [ ] Medical and dental insurance cards

- ☐ Prescription and over the counter medication
- ☐ Medical identification bracelet
- ☐ Medical information – 911 Card
- ☐ Physician's note outlining medical issues/food allergies
- ☐ Vitamins
- ☐ Thermometer
- ☐ Glucose tablets
- ☐ Chef cards
- ☐ _____
- ☐ _____

Carry-on luggage

- ☐ Important documents - passports, driver's license, birth certificate, visa, confirmations
- ☐ Medication
- ☐ Updated photo of your child
- ☐ Autism wallet card
- ☐ Starbrite Traveler Card
- ☐ Cares Seatbelt
- ☐ Wipes
- ☐ Change of clothing
- ☐ Airplane sheet cover
- ☐ Maps and travel directions
- ☐ Accessible maps/guide books
- ☐ Public transportation accessible stations and schedule
- ☐ Accessible cab information
- ☐ Important phone numbers of special providers
- ☐ _____
- ☐ _____

Toiletries

- ☐ Shampoo/conditioner
- ☐ Body wash
- ☐ Hairbrush/comb
- ☐ Deodorant

- ☐ Toothbrush/toothpaste
- ☐ Floss
- ☐ Blow dryer/hot iron
- ☐ Shaving items
- ☐ Antibacterial hand sanitizer
- ☐ Sunscreen
- ☐ Insect repellant
- ☐ Glasses/case/extra screws/tools
- ☐ Contacts/solution
- ☐ _____
- ☐ _____

Electronics/cameras

- ☐ Cell phone & charger/car charger
- ☐ Camera & charger
- ☐ Memory cards
- ☐ Camera batteries
- ☐ Video recorder/battery/charger/memory card
- ☐ Laptop & charger
- ☐ iPod & charger
- ☐ Headphones
- ☐ Portable DVD player and DVD's/cord/charger
- ☐ Surge protector
- ☐ GPS/power cord
- ☐ Safety tracking devices
- ☐ _____
- ☐ _____

Fun Bag

- ☐ Snacks
- ☐ Travel games
- ☐ Coloring books, crayons, stickers
- ☐ Travel journal
- ☐ Favorite blanket
- ☐ Handheld games

- ☐ Playing cards
- ☐ Earplugs
- ☐ Headset
- ☐ Sensory toys
- ☐ Puzzle books
- ☐ Audio books
- ☐ Magnetic drawing devices
- ☐ Special comfort items
- ☐ Audio-video items
- ☐ Stories
- ☐ Schedules
- ☐ _____
- ☐ _____

Service animal or pets

- ☐ Documentation (service animal)
- ☐ Food/bowls
- ☐ Medicine for pet
- ☐ Favorite toy
- ☐ Leash
- ☐ Treats
- ☐ _____
- ☐ _____

Miscellaneous

- ☐ Umbrella
- ☐ Collapsible cooler
- ☐ Sewing kit
- ☐ Safety pins
- ☐ Sunglasses
- ☐ Large plastic bags
- ☐ Ziplock bags
- ☐ Flashlight
- ☐ Penlight/lanyard
- ☐ Higher watt light bulb

☐ Extension cord

☐ _____

☐ _____

Go to starbritetravel.com to download this form.

It's not the destination that matters.
It's the change of scene.
-- Brian Eno

DESTINATION ARRIVAL

Congratulations! You made it to your destination. Now it is time for fun and relaxation. You planned a vacation to meet your child's needs and everyone's interests. Make sure you take time for yourself to enjoy the vacation and get some much needed relaxation. However, before hitting the pool:

- Discuss vacation safety rules calmly and firmly. Pay attention to any new safety issues you did not anticipate (e.g., there is an air conditioner in the hotel room window) and create new rules for those issues. Refer to Safety in Chapter 3.
- Post your child's countdown calendar to show the vacation days and activities.
- Post the morning and evening routine checklist.
- Create an activity schedule/story for the next day's activities if you did not already do so.
- Plan some time for yourself (e.g., schedule a massage, facial).

Depending on your child's special needs, you may need to:
- Speak with hotel staff about your child and provide them with a special needs card outlining your child's disability.
- Introduce family members and your child to the staff at the resort, hotel, B&B, or cruise ship.
- Explain to your child that these are the people he should go to for help if he is lost. Refer to the "Who Am I and Where Would You See Me?" activity in Safety, Chapter 3.
- Inform the hotel staff if your child tends to wander and to immediately notify you if they see your child wandering. Provide staff with your cell number.

- Safe proof your room. Refer to Safety in Chapter 3.
- Provide your child with an orientation of the room/ lobby area.
- Check if supplies/special equipment were delivered to your room (e.g., bedrails, shower bench, alert kits, refrigerator, hemodialysis equipment, medical supplies).
- Speak with the restaurant chef to assure special dietary needs are in place.
- Refrigerate medications, special foods, and/or beverages.

When visiting an attraction, remember to:
- Bring your child's activity schedule and any relevant stories.
- Review relaxation techniques.
- Take a picture of your child before leaving for handy reference if your child becomes separated from you. Immediately show the picture to staff members, security, and police officers at the attraction should it become necessary.
- Review safety rules. Refer to Safety in Chapter 3.
- Identify a safe meeting location for older children in the event they become separated from you. If this is your first time visiting this attraction, you may have to wait until you arrive at the destination to designate a meeting place. Walk your child to the area and show him exactly where to stand if lost.

While vacationing:
- Read a local newspaper, speak with your hotel concierge or tourism bureau to obtain discount coupons to attractions, and learn about "special events" happening in the area (e.g. parades, festivals, carnivals).
- Try something different – taste new foods, learn how to snorkel, ski, or zipline.
- Purchase something as a keepsake/memorabilia.

- Have your child collect different coins or bills as memorabilia.
- Collect brochures and other materials to help your child remember the trip, share his vacation with others when he returns home, and/or to make a scrapbook about his vacation.
- Plan for down time by eating lunch or dinner in a park or on the beach.
- Take advantage of spa amenities.
- Socialize with other adults on the trip.
- Take time to relax.
- Have breakfast foods for dinner - kids love bacon, eggs, and waffles.
- Have your child mail a post card to a family member and friends.
- Give your child his own disposable camera so he can take lots of photos to share with his teachers, friends, classmates, and relatives when he returns home.
- Do something special with each of your children alone (i.e. pick up shells at the beach, have ice-cream together, read a book).
- Use strategies you developed in Chapter 3 to prepare your child for activities –remember to use your child's schedules, stories, cartoons, and visual scripts.
- Reinforce your child's appropriate behavior
- **HAVE FUN!**

On the day before going home:
- Print off boarding passes.
- Confirm any special accommodations that need to be secured at the airport (e.g., transfers, equipment, special meals).
- Arrange for rented medical supplies/equipment to be returned to company.

CONCLUSION

Now that you have read *Starbrite Traveler: A Travel Resource for Parents of Children with Special Needs*, we hope you are feeling inspired to plan to travel with your family and empowered to deal with any challenging behaviors or special provisions that are required. Use this book as an ongoing resource for planning, preparing, and traveling.

This book is an evolving tool for your reference and to adapt to your child's needs, as he gets older, develops more skills, and your vacation needs change. Practice Dry Run strategies all year to help your child gain the skills to make travel a rewarding experience.

Depending on your family's needs, you may not be ready to take a vacation this year. If you are unable to travel this year, go on a day or weekend jaunt to prepare your child for traveling in the future.

Remember Emma and the happiness her entire family felt when she realized her dream of visiting Cinderella's castle. Their experience illustrates the benefits of travel and the possibilities for families to travel with a child with special needs. Disney was magical for Emma and her family. She still smiles as she looks at the photos of her vacation. As Emma's mother said, "The struggles fade, but the memories will last a lifetime."

Planning Emma's trip has left lasting memories for us as well. We consider ourselves fortunate to have shared in Emma's dream. Travel is no longer considered unobtainable for Emma and her family. We fulfilled our goal to help Emma take her dream vacation. We hope our book provides you with information to help your family travel.

One final note, travel with children requires a good sense of humor, patience, flexibility, and a "roll with the flow" attitude. Recognize that you may need to be more lenient when on vacation. There are certain privileges your child may have on vacation that he will not have at home. You may want to let your child have a treat before dinner rather than after, or stay up later to watch the fireworks, or a show. All of this comes with traveling and is great fun for kids.

With this in mind, remember the benefits of travel are invaluable for children with special needs.

The best vacations are the ones when your family is laughing together and having fun. These are the memories we all remember.

As you plan and take your vacation, please share your story with us. Your experience and suggestions will help us guide more families to successful travel. Have a wonderful vacation and YES, You Can Take That Trip!

Please contact us at starbritetraveler@gmail.com

APPENDICES

Appendix 1

Starbrite Traveler Card

★★★★★★★★★★★★★★★★★★★★★★★★★★★★★★★★★★★★★
★   ★
★ **My child is a S.T.A.R.brite traveler** ★
★ ★
★ Please show ★
★ *-Sensitivity:* My child is the same as you but with a disability. ★
★ *-Tolerance:* Understand if my child does not act or look like you. ★
★ *-Awareness:* Ask questions if you want to know more about ★
★ my child. ★
★ *-Respect:* My child is a human being with feelings. ★
★ ★
★★★★★★★★★★★★★★★★★★★★★★★★★★★★★★★★★★★★★

Appendix 2

Heat Safety

If you will be vacationing in a warm climate and/or plan to be involved in strenuous activities, your family may be at risk for a heat illness. Heat illness is broken down into two categories: Heat exhaustion, a condition that is caused by lack of body fluids and electrolytes due to being overheated and heat stroke, a condition when the internal body temperature rises due to body not being able to cool itself.

The following information comes directly from material prepared and distributed by Safe Kids USA (www.safekids.org). We thank Safe Kids USA for allowing us to provide you with their valuable information.

Defeat the Heat

What is dehydration?

Dehydration is the excessive loss of fluids from the body. It occurs when the total amount of water lost through sweating, urination, diarrhea, and/or vomiting is greater than the fluids taken in. A child with severe dehydration must be hospitalized to receive intravenous fluids.

What are the signs of dehydration and *heat exhaustion*?

Dehydration places children at risk for serious conditions like heat illnesses such as heat exhaustion and heat stroke.

Early signs of dehydration may include:	Early signs of heat exhaustion may include:
Thirst	Nausea
Dry or sticky mouth	Feeling faint or dizzy
Headache	Heavy sweating
Muscle cramping	Rapid, weak heartbeat
Irritability	Dark-colored urine
Extreme fatigue	Cool, moist, pale skin
Weakness	Cramps

Dizziness	Headache
Decreased performance	Fatigue

How to prevent dehydration
- **Drink before activity:** 12 ounces of fluid 30 minutes before activity begins
- **Drink during activity:**
- Children under 90 pounds: 5 ounces every 20 minutes
- Children over 90 pounds: 9 ounces every 20 minutes
- **Drink after activity:** Drink every 20 minutes during the first hour after the activity to make up for fluid loss.

What to do when dehydration and heat illness occurs
Treatment of dehydration and heat illness should take place immediately. Depending on the severity of the situation, seek medical attention from a certified athletic trainer or dial 911 for Emergency Medical Services.
- Move the child to a cool place.
- Have the child drink a glass of cool, lightly salted water or a sports drink, such as Gatorade.
- Raise the child's legs 8-12 inches.
- Sponge the child's head, face and trunk with cool, wet cloths.
- Fan the child.
- Keep the child from physical activity for the remainder of the day.

Comparison of Heat Illnesses
Heat Stroke
(The most severe and life –threatening)
- Dry, flushed hot skin
- Very high body temperature
- No sweating
- Life-threatening

Heat Exhaustion
(Less critical, but requires prompt attention)
- Moist, pale, cool skin
- Normal or sub-normal temperature
- Heavy sweating
- Serious, but not life-threatening

Appendix 3

Resources

Cruise Lines

Cruise Lines International Association (CLIA)

CLIA is the world's largest cruise association and is dedicated to promote all measures that foster a safe, secure and healthy cruise ship environment, educate, train its travel agent members, and promote and explain the value, desirability and affordability of the cruise vacation experience. CLIA was actively involved in preparing guidelines that address design and operation features for accommodation of person with disabilities.

CLIA provides a "Special Interest Guide for Wheelchair Travelers" which can be found on their website. This chart addresses the accessibility of cabins, restrooms, hallways, decks, and public rooms throughout each individual ship. Contact information: 1-800-327-9501 ext. 70025 or www.cruising.org/vacation/shipfinder. If you cannot find what you are looking for on the CLIA website, contact the Access departments for the specific cruise line. A disability specialist will provide you with information about special accommodations needed while cruising. There are many cruise lines that offer accommodation. We provide contact information for five cruise lines:

Carnival   1-800-438-6744 ext. 70025

Celebrity   1-866-592-7225

Disney   1-407-566-3602

Norwegian   1-305-436-4000

Royal Caribbean   1-800-722-5472 ext. 34492

Equipment and Supplies

The following are a sample of equipment and supply companies. Contact your physician or medical provider for any suggestions or recommendations. We do not endorse any company

Care Vacations

Provider of mobility scooters for adults, collapsible wheelchairs, oxygen rentals and other special needs equipment for cruise passengers with disabilities and aging travelers.
Contact information: 1- 877-478-7827 or http://carevacations.com

Dialysis at Sea Cruises

Specializes in the treatment of hemodialysis care while on-board cruise ships. Dialysis at Sea Cruises provides a renal care specialist team consisting of a nephrologist, dialysis nurse and certified technicians. Representatives at Dialysis at Sea report sailing on select cruises with Royal Caribbean, Holland America, and Celebrity Cruise Lines.
Contact information: 1-800-544-7604 or www.dialysisatsea.com

Special Needs at Sea

Special Needs Group, Inc. is a global provider of wheelchair rentals, scooter rentals, oxygen rentals and other special needs equipment rentals. Recommended by the world's major cruise lines for superior service and value, Special Needs Group also services guests visiting hotels, resorts, theme parks and convention centers.
Contact information: 1-800-513-4515 or www.specialneedsatsea. com

Food Allergies

The Food Allergy and Anaphylaxis Network (FAAN™)

Provides information, programs and resources about food allergies. Its Medical Advisory Board reviews FAAN's educational materials.
Contact information: 1-800-929-4040 or www.foodallergy.org

Allergy Free Table

Provides information about food allergies to help educate those who have food allergies, and those who are involved with individual with food allergies through the Web site, books, and on-line courses. Download and print from the Allergy Free Table Web site, pre-made chef cards for the following food allergies: peanuts, tree nuts, dairy, shellfish, fish, seafood, eggs, wheat, soy and gluten free intolerance. Contact information: 1-970-599-1076 or www.allergyfreetable.com

Health

American Lung Association

For information on traveling with a medical issue pertaining to a lung disease contact the American Lung Association. Contact information: 1-800-586-4872 or www.lungusa.org

Department of Health and Human Resources

Department provides travel health information worldwide. Contact information: www.cdc.gov

Hospitals World Wide

Locate the nearest hospital near your destination. Hospitals World Wide includes over 15,000 entries of hospitals and health clinics throughout the world. This on-line directory includes a road map and directions to the facility. Contact information: www.hospitalsworldwide.com

International Association for Medical Assistance for Travelers

This association offers world wide medical assistance including medical I.D. cards, a directory of English-speaking physicians and 24 hour world climate charts provided free to members. The charts list climate, suggested clothing, and sanitary conditions in 1,120 cities throughout the world. Contact information: 1-716-754-4883 or www.iamat.org

International Society of Travel Medicine
The International Society of Travel Medicine (ISTM) promotes healthy and safe travel. In cooperation with health care providers, academic centers, the travel industry and the media, ISTM advocates and facilitates education, service, and research activities in the field of travel medicine. The directory is an international listing of ISTM member travel medicine clinics that offer pre-travel immunizations, counseling and medicines to help protect travelers while traveling internationally. Most clinics also provide care to travelers if needed upon their return. There are currently clinics located in 65 countries included in the directory.
Contact information: www.istm.org

Medical Alert Card/911
Medical Alert Card/911 – a flash drive that stores your important medical information and connects to any computer for ease of access and viewing of your medical information.
Contact information: 1-732-865-6874 or http://911medicalid.com

Legislature

American Disability Act (ADA)
The ADA of 1990 gives civil rights protections to individuals with disabilities similar to those provided to individuals on the basis of race, color, sex, national origin, age, and religion. It guarantees equal opportunity for individual with disabilities in public accommodations, employment, transportation, state and local government services, and telecommunications.

Title I of the law covers place of employment: Title II state and local governments. Title IV covers telecommunications for the deaf and hard of hearing, and Title V covers miscellaneous items. The section of ADA that deals with public facilities is Title III. Facilities covered as listed by ADA are the following: places of lodging, exhibition, or entertainment, public gathering, public display or collection, recreation, and exercise; private educational institutions; establishments serving food of drink; service establishments; stations

used for specific public transportation; and social service center establishments.
Contact information: 1-800-514-0301/TTY 1-800-514-0383 or www. ada.gov/pubs/ada.htm

Air Carrier Access Act

This regulation was published in 1990 and has been amended several times. It prohibits discrimination on the basis of disability in air travel. The Department of Transportation has a rule defining the rights of passengers and the obligations of airlines under this law. The rule applies to all flights of U.S. airlines and to flights to or from the United States by foreign airlines. For a summary of main points of the rule (Title 14 CFR Part 382) includes: responsibility of travelers, air carriers, airport operations, and contractors.
Contact information: http://airconsumer.dot.gov/publications/ disabled.htm

Safety

Child Aviation Restraint System (CARES)

CARES is a safety harness designed specifically for airplanes. This device hooks onto the airplane seat and provides the same level of safety as a car seat. It weighs one pound.
Contact information: 1- 602-850-2850 or www.amsafe.com

ID Non-permanent tattoos

For children with sensory sensitivity purchase a prepared, washable, non-permanent tattoo that has ID information.
Contact information: www.tattooswithapurpose.com

ID PUP System of Identification

Apparel and tag identification system that helps first responders and others identify lost or stranded children.
Contact information: 1-732-865-6874 or www.IDPUP.com

Travel Resources

Access-Able Travel Source
Provides information on accessible facilities, accommodations, and services, including rentals of vans and medical equipment.
Contact information: www.access-able.com

National Parks
A free lifetime access pass for national parks is available to U.S. citizens or permanent residents of the U.S that have been medically determined to have a permanent disability.
Contact information: http://www.nps.gov/findapark/passes.htm

Aviation Consumer Protection and Reinforcement
An on-line resource designed to offer travelers with disability information about the Air Carrier Access Act (ACAA).
Contact information: http://www.airconsumer.ost.dot.gov/publications/horizons.htm

Society for Accessible Travel and Hospitality (SATH)
Maintains lists of tour operators and travel agencies with experience in serving travelers with disabilities.
Contact information: 1-212-447-7284 or www.sath.org

Starry Night Travel, LLC
Full service travel agency that focuses on travel for children and adults with special needs.
Contact information: www.starrynighttravel.biz or starbritetravel.com

Transportation

Air Travel
Transportation Security Administration (TSA)/
TSA Cares Help Line
Prior to air travel, be sure to review TSA regulations for equipment requirements, acceptable wheelchair dimensions, medical portable

electronic devices, and regulations about batteries, ventilators, or respirators. TSA Cares is a helpline designed to assist travelers with disabilities and medical conditions. Contact the Cares hotline with questions pertaining to screening policies, procedures and what to expect at the security checkpoint. It is recommended that passengers call approximately 72 hours ahead of travel so that TSA Cares has the opportunity to coordinate checkpoint support with a TSA Customer Service Manager located at the airport if necessary.
Contact information: 1-855-787-2227 or http://www.tsa.gov/traveler-information/travelers-disabilities-and-medical-conditions

U.S. Department of Transportation (DOT)
The toll-free hotline provides information about the rights of air travelers with disabilities. You can also call the hotline if you have a time-sensitive disability-related issue that needs to be addressed in "real time." The line is staffed from 7 a.m. to 11 p.m. Eastern time, seven days a week.
Contact information: 1-800-778-4838/TDD 1-800-455-9880 or http://airconsumer.ost.dot.gov/hotline.htm

Train Travel

Amtrak
Free accessibility guides are available in alternate formats – Braille, large print, audio-tape and diskette. Amtrak also offers discounts to persons with a physical or mental disability.
Contact information: www.Amtrak.com, 1-800-872-7245 or TTY 1-800-523-6590

Wheelchair Accessible Vehicles

Accessible Vans of America
Contact information: 1-866-224-1750 or www.accessiblevans.com

Wheelchair Getaways, Inc.
Contact information: 1-800-642-2042 or http://www.wheelchairget-aways.com/

Wheelers Accessible Vans Contact information: 1- 800-456-1371 or http://www.wheelers.com/

Appendix 4

What Does Research Say About the Strategies in Dry Run?
We carefully chose strategies to address travel concerns discussed in Chapter 3. Empirical evidence supports the use of these strategies to address a variety of needs with learners with diverse disabilities. The strategies have not necessary been applied to the travel concerns discussed here or to learners with each of the disabilities discussed in this book, but, as we illustrated, they could be. Carefully consider the strategies and how best to apply them to your situation for your child. For additional information, see the references described here.

Behavior Specific Praise Statements
Behavior Specific Praise Statements have been demonstrated to improve classroom performance for children with a range of disabilities (Hester, Hendrickson, & Gable, 2009), (Sutherland, Wehby, & Copeland, 2000), (Thompson, Marchant, Anderson, Prater, & Gibb, 2012).

Choice Making
Choice making improves appropriate behavior and decrease challenging behavior in children with a variety of disabilities (Jolivette, Ridgley, White 2013). Choice making is an established intervention identified in the National Standards Report of Evidence-Based Practice Guidelines for Autism Spectrum Disorders, (National Autism Center, 2009).

Modeling
Modeling and video modeling have been used in a variety of settings to teach a number of different skills to children with disabilities (Charlop-Christy, Le, & Freeman, 2000). In a review of video modeling, (Bellini and Akullian, 2007) concluded video modeling is effective to address a variety of skills for learners with autism Modeling is an established intervention identified in the National Standards Report of Evidence-Based Practice Guidelines for Autism

Spectrum Disorders, (National Autism Center, 2009). Modeling is effective to address:

- Transitioning
- Communication skills
- Interpersonal skills
- Personal responsibility
- Play skills
- Problem behaviors

Visual Supports

A number of the strategies in Chapter 3 are examples of visual supports including stories, Comic Strip Conversations, scripts, and schedules. According to the National Standards Report of Evidence-Based Practice Guidelines for Autism Spectrum Disorders, (National Autism Center, 2009) visual supports are effective strategies to address:

- Transitions
- Self-regulation
- Aggressive/disruptive behaviors
- Independence
- On-task behaviors
- Predictability
- Reduce anxiety
- Communication
- Social behaviors
- Rules

One type of cartooning, **Comic Strip Conversations,** was developed by (Carol Gray, 1994). Some research suggests this approach is promising (Pierson, Glaeser, & Fritschmann, 2003).

Comic Strip Conversations can be used to:

- Convey important information
- Problem-solve and conflict resolution
- Learn social skills
- Follow simple rules
- Communicate perspectives, feelings, and ideas

Visual schedules are also referred to as picture schedules or activity schedules (McClannahan & Krantz, 2010). Schedules are identified as an established intervention in the National Standards Report of Evidence-Based Practice Guidelines for Autism Spectrum Disorders (National Autism Center, 2009). Schedules may help improve:

- Independence
- Performance of tasks/steps on the schedule
- Active participation
- Appropriate behavior

Scripts are appropriate for use with children with communication, social, and cognitive needs (Ganz, 2007). Scripts are identified as an emerging intervention in the National Standards Report of Evidence-Based Practice Guidelines for Autism Spectrum Disorders (National Autism Center, 2009).

There are a number of examples of stories in the literature. Perhaps the best known example is Carol Gray's Social Stories™, a strategy for teaching children social skills (Gray, 1993). Social stories™ or similar stories that involve a visual presentation of a description of a situation in story format have a growing evidence-base suggesting they are a promising strategy (National Autism Center, 2009; Sansosti, Powell-Smith, & Kincaid, 2004; Test, Richter, Knight, & Spooner, 2011). Stories may be effective to address:

- Interpersonal skills
- Communication skills
- Social behavior
- Choice and play skills
- Understanding emotions

- Mealtime skills
- Self-regulation
- Problem behavior

Progressive Muscle Relaxation

Progressive muscle relaxation is one component of effective behavioral packages to address challenging behavior and teach more appropriate behavior (National Autism Center, 2009). Relaxation techniques help manage sensory overload, anxiety, and transitioning.

Appendix 5

Travel Budget Worksheet

TRANSPOR-TATION	AMOUNT	LODGING	AMOUNT	ADDI-TIONAL COSTS	AMOUNT
Airfare		Hotels/ Motels/B&B		Medical Supplies	
Transporta-tion to/from Airport		Cruise		Materials Shipped	
Long Term Parking at Airport		All-Inclusive		Alert Kit	
Taxi Fare		Campsite/ Cabin Rental		Oxygen	
Train/ Subway Fare		Phone/ Internet Charge		Rental Vans	
Rental Car		Other		Equip-ment Rental	
Gasoline				Nursing Service	
Tolls					
Other					
TOTAL		TOTAL		TOTAL	

FOOD BEVERAGES	AMOUNT	ACTIVITIES ATTRAC-TIONS	AMOUNT	PUR-CHASE AT HOME	AMOUNT
Meals (Breakfast/ Lunch/ Dinner)		Excursions Sightseeing Entertain-ment		Camera Memory Card	
Snacks/ Beverage		Rental Equipment		Guide-books Language Dictionar-ies	
Groceries		Museums Amusement Parks Aquariums		Road Atlas GPS	
Special Formula Food				Luggage	
TOTAL		TOTAL		TOTAL	

EXPENSES ON VACA-TION	AMOUNT	INSURANCE	AMOUNT	MISCEL-LANEOUS	AMOUNT
Personal Needs (Toiletries)		Travel Insurance		Passport Fees	
Spending Money (Gifts, Souvenirs)					
				Childcare Costs	
				Kennel Costs	
TOTAL		TOTAL		TOTAL	

Go to starbritetravel.com to download this form.

Appendix 6

Permission to Travel Letter

Date: _____

I/We _____ and _____
parent./guardian name   parent/guardian name

authorize my child(ren)_____
name of child/children

to travel to _____ on _____
destination   date of travel

with _____ returning on _____.
accompanying adult(s)   date of return

Airline:_____ Flight #: _____

Cruise Line: _____ Ship: _____

Other: _____

Signed by Parent(s) _____

Name: _____

Address: _____

Telephone/Contact: _____

TO BE FILLED OUT BY A NOTARY PUBLIC:

The above parties signed and sworn before me on

_____
month/day/year

Notary Public Signature:_____

Notary Public in and for the County of _____ and the
State of _____

(Notary Seal or Stamp)

Go to starbritetravel.com to download this form.

Appendix 7

Money Saving Tips

- Club memberships like AAA, Costco Travel Club and Sam's Travel Club can often save you money on attractions and related travel.
- Be careful not to jump on the first deal you see. Carefully calculate the savings. The 30% off the entire hotel stay may be less costly than the 4th night free.
- Find hotels that offer free Wi-Fi for Internet access.
- Enroll in a hotel loyalty program where you can accrue points through hotel stays and redeem them for room upgrades and free night stays.
- Eat meals at restaurants or hotels where children eat free.
- Use coupons. Look for discount coupons for lodging, attractions and food in local papers and on the Internet.
- Take advantage of multi-day passes at the attractions.
- Search E-bay for travel coupons and discounts on entrance fees to amusement parks, science centers, museums, car rentals.
- If you are a member of a science museum that is part of the Association of Science Technology Centers, you can get free admission to its affiliate at other destinations throughout the country.
- Museums, zoos and botanical gardens often have reciprocal privileges with facilities throughout the country; consider buying a counterpart membership near your home.
- In Washington D.C there is free admission to all of the Smithsonian Museums, National Monuments, National Zoos, and National Art Galleries.
- Buy an Entertainment Book, filled with discount coupons for restaurants, attractions and entertainment in the city you plan on visiting for a lengthy visit, short visits may not be cost effective. www.entertainment.com.

- Go to goldstar.com for discount tickets to shows and events in many major cities.
- If you plan on exploring the city for more than one day, a City Pass is the best deal. Receive approximately 50% off certain attractions, receive a map and skip waiting in ticket lines. www.citypass.com
- Visit BroadwayBox.com for ticket discounts.
- Refillable bottles are great for water as the price of bottled water is high. Add flavored packets to water to make a quick drink. Note: check with the facility you are planning to see if you are permitted to bring in refillable bottles. Eat before you arrive at the airport as food and drink can be costly.

GLOSSARY

Accessible guide maps – maps that show accessible features of the facility

Accommodations – lodging

American Disability Act (ADA) – gives civil rights protection to individuals with disabilities

Adaptive skiing – skiing using special equipment

Advanced imagining technology machine – a machine used by TSA to scan passengers for banned metallic and non-metallic objects. A passenger must stand still for several seconds in the center of the machine with their arms raised over their heads. This machine displays an image of the passenger

Airplane specific wheelchair - a narrow wheelchair that fits through the aisles on an airplane

Alpine skiing – downhill skiing

All suites – rooms with a separate sleeping and living area

Amenities – comforts and conveniences

Behavior Specific Praise Statements (BSPS) – Behavior Specific Praise Statements (BSPS) are positive statements intended to reinforce desired behavior

Bi-skis – a bucket style seat with two skis underneath it

Braille – a formal written language for individuals with visual impairments where raised symbols are used to represent letters and words

Bulkhead – seats that give more room in front of a passenger on an airplane

Campground – an outdoor area for setting up camp

Closed caption television – dialogue from a television show appears in a black box at the bottom of the screen

Cochlear implants –electronic hearing devices for people with profound deafness or severe hearing loss who do not benefit from a hearing aid

Concierge – staff member of a hotel or cruise ship whose function is to provide information and services to guests

Cross contamination –when one food comes into contact with another food and their proteins mix

Cross country skiing – skiing across the countryside

Deluxe accommodations – luxurious hotel

Disembarking – getting off the ship

Distracters – a person or thing that distracts the child's attention

Embarkation point – where you board the ship

Epinephrine pen – a medical device used to deliver a measured dose of Epinephrine (adrenaline), most often a treatment for acute allergic reaction

Extended stay hotel – hotel with option to stay for weeks/months; amenities such as housekeeping service, laundry services are available

Fade – decrease level of assistance to complete a task or activity

Federal Aviation Administration (FAA) – agency of the federal government responsible for ensuring the safety of civil aviation

First class – a very good to excellent hotel

Guest assistance pass - a pass that provides assistance or special provisions for individuals with disabilities. The pass may provide a different entrance to access rides with possibly a shorter line and a shaded spot and a seat up front at shows

Hearing loops – a thin strand of copper wire radiating electromagnetic signals that can be picked up by a tiny receiver built into special hearing aids and cochlear implants

Medical evacuation – transfer from cruise ship to hospital via helicopter or ground transportation

Mono-skis – a bucket style seat with a single ski underneath

Motorized equipment – equipment with a motor (e.g., jet ski)

Non-motorized equipment – equipment without a motor (e.g., snorkel, boogie board)

Orientation tours – a tour of the public spaces

Ports of call – any of the ports at which a ship will be stopping on a cruise

Priority boarding – first group of people to board a ship or airplane

Private muster drill - a safety demonstration conducted by members of the ship's staff that instructs passengers on the use of a life preserver and other important safety information – individuals that have difficulty with loud noises or crowds will be taken to an alternate quiet location on the ship

Prompt – a cue given to help remember what to say or do

Recreational Vehicle (RV) – a large vehicle used for camping

Reinforcers – a reward given to maintain or increase the future likelihood of that behavior

Respite – a short rest or relief

Rough terrain – irregular surface

Shore excursion – organized land based trips on a cruise

Shuttle vehicle – a public transport bus service designed to transport people between points – usually from airport to hotel

Sliders – a type of ski mounted to a walker

Special provisions – appropriate supplies and devices for individuals with special needs, i.e. wheelchair accessibility, adaptive equipment, dietary needs, transportation, medical supplies, and oxygen

Special equipment – wheelchair, walker, TTY devices

Stabilizers – devices that extend from both sides of the ship to minimize roll

Standard – services usually found on most cruise ships and hotels

Stateroom – a cabin on a ship

Support staff – reservation desk, concierge, valet, and housekeeping

Telecommunication device (TTY) – special device that enables an individual who is deaf or hard of hearing to use the telephone to communicate by allowing them to type text

Tenders – a small boat that transports passengers from the cruise ship to the shore

Transitions – a change from one activity to another

Trip insurance – insurance that is intended to cover medical expenses and other losses incurred when traveling

Transportation Security Administration (TSA) – agency responsible for safeguarding U.S. transportation systems and insuring safety

Visual/tactile alert kits - kits that include special equipment that can be installed in your hotel room or cabin to ensure that individuals who are deaf or hard of hearing will be alerted if someone knocks on the door, the telephone rings, or a smoke detector goes off

REFERENCES/BIBLIOGRAPHY

Anderson, C., Law, J K., Daniel, A., Rice, C, Mandell, D.S. Hagopian, L., & Law, P.A. (2012). Occurrence & family impact of elopement in children with autism spectrum disorder. *Pediatrics,* 130 (5), 870-877.

Ayres, K., & Langone, J. (2005). Strategy and instruction with video for students with autism: A review of the literature. *Education and Training in Developmental Disabilities*, *40*, 183-196.

Banda, D., Grimmett, E., & Hart, S. (2009). Activity schedule: Helping children with autism spectrum disorders in general education classrooms manage transition issues. *Teaching Exceptional Children*, *41*(4), 16-21.

Banda, D., Matuszn R., & Turkan S. (2007). Video modeling strategies to enhance appropriate behaviors in children with autism spectrum disorders. *Teaching Exceptional Children*, *39*(6), 47-51.

Bellini, S., & Akullian, J. (2007). A meta-analysis of video modeling and video-self-modeling interventions for children and adolescents with autism spectrum disorders. *Exceptional Children*, *73*(3), 264-287.

Buggey, T. (2007). A picture is worth...video self-modeling applications at school and home. *Journal of Positive Behavior Interventions*, *9*(2), 151-158.

Carr, S., & Punzo, R. (1993). The effects of self-monitoring of academic accuracy and productivity on the performance of students with behavioral disorders. *Behavioral Disorder*, *18*(4), 241-251.

Charlop-Christy, C. M., Le L., & Freeman K. (2000). A comparison of videoing modeling with in-vivo modeling for teaching children with autism. *Journal of Autism and Developmental Disorders*, *30*, 537-553.

Edwards, C. (1993). *Classroom management and discipline*. New York, NY: Macmillam.

Fjortoft, I. (2001). The natural environment as a playground for children: The impact of outdoor play activities in pre-primary school children. *Early Childhood Education Journal*, *29*(2), 111-117.

Franzone, E., & Collet-Klingenberg, L. (2008). *Overview of video modeling*. Madison, WI: The National Professional Development Center on Autism Spectrum Disorders, Waisman Center, University of Wisconsin.

Fujiura, G. (1998). Demography of family households. *American Journal on Mental Retardation, 103*, 225-235.

Ganz, J. (2007). Using visual script interventions to address communication skills. *Teaching Exceptional Children, 40*(2), 54-58.

Glaeser, B., Pierson M., & Fristschmann N. (2003). Comic strip conversation: A positive behavioral support strategy. *Teaching Exceptional Children, 36*, 14-19.

Grandin, T. (2002, December). Teaching tips for children and adults with autism. *ASPEN Asperger Syndrome Education Network*. Retrieved November 18, 2012, from http://www.aspennj.org/

Grandin, T. (2006). *Thinking in pictures: My life with autism* (2nd ed.). New York, NY: Vintage Press.

Gray, C. (1994). *Comic strip conversations: Illustrated interactions that teach conversation skills to students with autism and related disorders*. Arlington, TX: Future Horizons.

Gray, C. A., & Garant, J. D. (1993). Social stories: Improving responses of students with autism with accurate social information. *Focus on Autism and Other Developmental Disabilities, 8*, 1-10.

Grimmett, E., & Hart, S. (2004). Activity schedules: Helping children with autism spectrum disorders in general education classrooms manage transition issues. *Teaching Exception Children, 41*(4), 16-21.

Heflin, T., & Simpson, R. (1998). Interventions for children and youth with autism: Prudent choices in a world of exaggerated claims and empty promises. *Focus on Autism and Other Developmental Disabilities, 13*, 194-211.

Hester, P. P., Hendrickson, J. M., & Gable, R. A. (2012). Forty years later - the value of praise, ignoring, and rules for preschoolers at risk for behavior disorders. *Education and Treatment of Children, 32*, 513-535.

Jolivette, K., Ridgley, R., & White, A.I. (n.d.). Choice-making strategies: Information for families. *Center for Effective Collaboration and*

Practice (CECP). Retrieved March 2, 2013, from http://cecp.air.org/familybriefs/

Kaplan, R., & Kaplan, S. (1989). *The experience of nature: A psychological perspective.* New York, NY: Cambridge University Press.

Kern, L., Ringdahl, J. E., Hilt, A., & Sterling-Turner, H. E. (2001). Linking self management procedures to functional analysis results. *Behavior Disorders, 26,* 214-266.

Kerr, S., & Durkin, K. (2004). Understanding of thought bubbles as mental representation in children with autism: Implications for theory of mind. *Journal of Autism and Developmental Disorders, 34,* 637-648.

Kroeger, S., Burton, C., Comarata, A., Combs, C., Hamm, C., & Hopkins, R. (2004). Student voice and critical reflection: Helping students at risk. *Teaching Exceptional Children, 36*(3), 50-57.

Kuo, F., & Taylor A. (2004). A potential national treatment for attention deficit/hyperactivity disorder: Evidence from a national study. *American Journal of Public Health, 94*(9), 1580-1586.

Lite, L. (n.d.). Breathing decreases anxiety. *Stress Free Kids.* Retrieved November 10, 2012, from www.stressfreekids.com

Marr, D., & Nackley, V. (2005). A new tool to improve participation for children with over-reproductive sensory modulation. *Sensory Integration Focus,* 8-9.

Maxim, G. W. (1997). *The very young: Developmental education for early years* (5th ed.). Saddle River, NJ: Merrill/Prentice Hall.

McClannahan, L. E., & Krantz, P. J. (2010). *Activity schedules for children with autism: Teaching independent behavior* (2nd ed.). Bethesda, MD: Woodbine House.

Moore, R. (1996). Compact nature: The role of playing and learning gardens on children's lives. *Journal of Therapeutic Horticulture, 8,* 72-82.

National Autism Center. (2009). *National Standards Report.* Randolph, MA: National Autism Center. Retrieved from http://www.nationalautismcenter.org/nsp/

Ogilivie, C. S. (2011). Step-by-step social skills instruction for students with autism spectrum disorder using video modeling and peer mentors. *Teaching Exceptional Children, 43*(6), 20-26.

Pierson, M. R., Glaeser, B. C., & Fritschmann, N. (2003). Comic strip conversation: A positive behavioral support strategy. *Teaching Exceptional Children, 36*(2), 14-19.

Relaxation techniques: Try these steps to reduce stress. (2011, May 19). *Mayo Clinic.* Retrieved October 5, 2012, from www.mayo-clinic.com

Sansosti, F. J., Powell-Smith, K. A., & Kincaid, D. (2004). A research synthesis of social story interventions for children with autism spectrum disorders. *Focus on Autism and Other Developmental Disabilities, 19,* 194-204.

Sutherland, K. S., Wehby, J. H., & Copeland, S. R. (2000). Effect of varying rates of behavior-specific praise on the on-task behavior of students with EBD. *Journal of Emotional and Behavioral Disorders, 8,* 2-8.

Strayer, D., Atchley, P., & Atchley R.A. (2012, April 23). Researchers find time in wild boosts creativity, insight, and problem solving. *Kansas University News Release.*

Swanson, H. L., Harris, K. R., & Graham, S. (2003). *Handbook of learning disabilities.* New York, NY: Guilford Press.

Test, D. W., Richter, S., Knight, V., & Spooner, F. (2011). A comprehensive review and meta-analysis of the Social Stories literature. *Focus on Autism and Other Developmental Disabilities, 26*(1), 49-62.

Thompson, M. T., Marchant, M., Anderson, D., Prater, M. A., & Gibb, G. (2012). Effects of tiered training on general educators' use of specific praise. *Education and Treatment of Children, 35,* 521-546.

Wells, N. M., & Evan, G. W. (2003). Nearby nature: A buffer of life stress among rural children. *Environment and Behavior, 35*(3), 311-330.

White, R. (2012, May 30). Welcome to the White Hutchinson Leisure & Learning Group Website. *White Hutchinson.* Retrieved September 10, 2012, from http://www.whitehutchinson.com/

Available June 2013

Starbrite Traveler: Destinations for Kids with Special Needs - East Coast Edition

Starbrite Traveler is an invaluable resource to help parents choose special needs friendly destinations along the East Coast of the United States. We look at the educational aspects of going on vacation and how to make your vacation a learning experience for your child. Enrich your child's life by traveling. The benefits of travel are abundant. Travel is fun, educational, broadens your child's sense of wonder, and strengthens family bonds.

You Will Find:

☆ *Special* needs friendly destinations for the entire family including zoos, museums, planetariums, amusement/theme parks, state and national parks along the East Coast.

☆ *Fun* activities and travel games to play with your child to enhance his reading, writing, math, science, communication, social and life skills on vacation and after vacation.

☆ *Accessible* accommodations, programs, and supports provided for children with special needs.

☆ *Special* programs for children with autism at various attractions.

☆ *Adaptive* ski resorts for children with autism, physical disabilities, and visual impairments.

☆ *Information* about large cities mass transit accessibility.

Discover the Beautiful East Coast with Your Family!

A portion of the proceeds of our books are donated to children's charities

Contact starbritetraveler@gmail.com or stabritetraveler.com to order your copy

West Coast and Midwest Editions Coming Spring 2014

STARBRITE Kids

I would like information on the following:

- ☐ Starbrite Kids Membership Club
    - ☐ Sirius level
    - ☐ Vega level
    - ☐ Rigel level

- ☐ Vacations with Starbrite Staff

- ☐ Special Vacation Promotions

- ☐ Speaking/Seminars

- ☐ Consulting

- ☐ On line correspondence with staff at Starbrite Traveler

- ☐ Other books and articles by Starbrite Traveler

Please visit www.starbritetraveler.com
Contact us at starbritetraveler@gmail.com

Starbrite Kids' Travel, LLC
P.O. Box 7445
Shrewsbury, New Jersey 07702

A portion of the proceeds of our books and travel are donated to children's charities

Starbrite Traveler: A Travel Resource for Parents of Children with Special Needs

What people are saying.....

"What an excellent resource for people looking to plan vacations that all members of their family will enjoy. The author provides a wealth of information on so many forms of travel but manages to keep it concise and user-friendly. Just what we all want when faced with the daunting task of selecting the right vacation destination for our loved ones. They also include thoughtful strategies to address specific issues that may arise when travelling with a child with special needs."

Andrea Morris, M.Ed., Education Consultant –
The Watson Institute, Pittsburgh, PA

"This book is a must have for families requiring special travel accommodations for their children. The checklists and tips provided throughout the book are extremely helpful. It is well organized, informative and provides all that is necessary for planning a successful trip".

John Andl, Ed.D. Principal – New Monmouth Elementary School

"From an unimaginable task to a remarkable adventure....Starbrite Traveler has made traveling and entertainment for families with special needs a stress-free experience."

Brenda Calderone, President Brick Township Special Education PTA

"An interesting and informative book for anyone with a special needs child. It is full of countless helpful tips and resources to help make traveling easier on both the child and the family."

Jenn Baumgarten, Parent of a child with special needs

"OUTSTANDING!! This comprehensive travel guide is a <u>must have</u> for <u>all!</u> Now dreams to explore can come true."

Maria Walsh, M.S.Ed., Special Education Teacher

ABOUT THE AUTHORS

Jesemine Jones and Ida Keiper are co-founders of the Starbrite Kids Program and Starry Night Travel, LLC, a travel agency that specializes in planning travel for families with a child with special needs. They have fifty years of combined experience educating children with a broad spectrum of disabilities.

Their dream of helping children with special needs began when they were in college studying to become special education teachers. Together, they have hosted workshops and participated in special needs conferences, published articles in magazines, as well as a series of articles online for Kidsville News! Their close friendship has continued over the last thirty years.

Ms. Jones earned a Masters of Social Work from Rutgers University as well as a B.A. in Special Education from Georgian Court University. She is currently a social worker in the New Jersey public school system. A former special education teacher, mental health therapist, lead counselor of a therapeutic foster care program, and team leader for an alternative high school for classified students, Ms. Jones has extensive experience working with children with special needs as well as their families. Ms. Jones lives in New Jersey with her husband and daughters.

Ms. Keiper is dually certified as Teacher of the Handicapped and Elementary Education. She earned a B.A. from Georgian Court University. Ms. Keiper, a highly qualified teacher, educated children with disabilities for thirty years in New Jersey public schools. She wrote district curriculum for special education, and acted as teacher coordinator for her department. Her compassion and professionalism earned her "Teacher of the Year." Over the years Ms. Keiper has fostered close relationships with her students and parents. She lives in New Jersey with her husband and two sons.

Emily A. Jones, Ph. D, BCBA-D, is an Assistant Professor in the Department of Psychology at Queens College. Dr. Jones teaches courses in applied behavior analysis and developmental disabilities. She also provides training and technical assistance to families, school districts, and other service providers to support children with developmental disabilities in inclusive settings. Dr. Jones's research involves the development and demonstration of interventions to address early emerging core deficits in young children with developmental disabilities such as autism and Down syndrome.

CPSIA information can be obtained at www.ICGtesting.com
Printed in the USA
LVOW01s1657070813

346786LV00019B/1136/P